Exploring the Media

Text, Industry, Audience

Barbara Connell

auteur

EXPLORING THE MEDIA

First published in 2008 by Auteur, The Old Surgery, 9 Pulford Road, Leighton Buzzard LU7 1AB
www.auteur.co.uk
Copyright © Auteur 2008

Design: Nikki Hamlett
Stills research and production assistance: Tom Cabot (www.ketchup-productions.co.uk)
Main cover image: Tom Barrance
Set by AMP Ltd, Dunstable, Bedfordshire
Printed and bound by Scotprint, Haddington, Scotland

British Library Cataloguing-in-Publication Data
A catalogue record for this book is available from the British Library

ISBN 978-1-903663-92-9 (paperback)
ISBN 978-1-903663-93-6 (cloth)

Contents

List of Contributors

BARBARA CONNELL is Subject Leader for Media Studies, Coleg Glan Hafren, Cardiff and Chief Examiner, A Level Media Studies, WJEC.

CHRISTINE BELL is Head of Media Studies, Heaton Manor School, Newcastle-upon-Tyne and is Principal Examiner, A Level Media Studies, WJEC.

VIVIENNE CLARK teaches Media and Film at Langley Park School for Boys, Beckenham, and was a Principal Examiner for AS/A Level Media Studies for one of the UK national awarding bodies.

COLIN DEAR is Head of Media Studies, Royal Russell School, Croydon, and is a Team Leader, A Level Media Studies, WJEC.

MANDY ESSEEN is Head of English, Cardiff High School, Cardiff, and is Principal Examiner, A Level Media Studies, WJEC.

WENDY HELSBY taught Media and Film at Queen Mary's College, Basingstoke and is also a tutor for the Open University.

NAOMI HODKINSON is Lecturer in Media Studies, Coleg Glan Hafren, Cardiff, and is an Examiner, A Level Media Studies, WJEC.

PIP JONES is Head of Media Studies, St David's Catholic College, Cardiff, and is an Examiner, A Level Media Studies, WJEC.

SAM WILLIAMS is Head of Media Studies, Croesyceiliog School, Cwmbran, and is an Examiner, A Level Media Studies, WJEC.

Editor's Introduction

Exploring the Media has been written by a group of practising teachers of Media Studies and reflects some of the recent changes in AS and A Levels in Britain. The book is based on what the writers see as the central concepts informing the study of the media: 'texts' (a general term to describe all products of the media), their audiences and the industries which produce them. We believe that these concepts are fundamental to a study of the media. But we think it is important not only to study products of the media – broadly by asking questions about their genre, narrative and the representation issues they raise – but also to ask questions about how those media products are shaped by the audiences they're produced for and the industries which produce them. It's only through considering all of those elements that we can begin to understand the role that the media may play in shaping the way we think and feel.

You will realise early on in your study of the media that the media do not just provide a 'window on reality', they provide us with representations of the world we live in – versions of that 'reality'. When you explore those representations, you will begin to see that representations are, at their simplest, images of 'reality' coupled with points of view about them. They are what the writers of this book refer to as 'ideological representations' – representations which incorporate attitudes, values and beliefs. Representations which are also influenced by the audiences they appeal to and the organisations which produced them. So, for example a television drama like *The Wire* – will give you a very different view of crime, the police and criminals from, for example, an episode of the popular crime series *Midsomer Murders*. That is partly to do with the fact that *Midsomer Murders* is produced by ITV1 for mainstream television viewing whereas *The Wire* was originally produced by HBO (Home Box Office, part of the massive Time Warner empire), who have a tradition of creating challenging dramas for an American pay-TV audience who like riskier television.

Expanding the concepts

So, thinking about media 'texts' in relation to their audiences and producers is important. Concepts and ideologies are however themselves changing as the media becomes ever more convergent. Consequently the way we relate to the media is changing so that we combine being audiences, in the traditional sense, for some media – like watching television or going to a film – with being interactive users, and often at the same time! For example, you may watch a television programme on your computer and simultaneously open up various interactive windows at the same time as emailing a friend.

The convergence within the media and the ways in which audiences are using – and relating – to it have several implications for the way we study 'texts'. We might, for example, think about the way we explore media texts by considering their genre – what kind of text they are, why genres have developed and how audiences and industries 'use' them. You could describe a television programme like *skins* as a 'teen drama', with more than a touch of soap, but you could also talk about it as a 'multiplatform' drama with viewers watching online or attending some of the parties it sponsored. Or you might be one of the many who produced their own scenes from it or picked up mobisodes or deleted scenes on mobile phones or the web. The 'kind' of programme you're studying has changed from being a simple television programme creating particular expectations in audiences and following particular 'rules' to a multiplatform experience.

Equally, you might think of how computer games are immersing us all in different kinds of narrative. At their simplest, game narratives are less about beginnings, middles and ends and more about following up different possibilities. The 'linear' narrative is often replaced by parallel and multi-layered narratives.

The book's structure: text, audiences/users and industry

The first section of the book introduces the concepts of genre, narrative and representation as the main ways of exploring the media and analysing texts. The section emphasises representation issues and starts to ask questions about how audiences and users respond to - and are potentially influenced by - those representations. You will find references to Stuart Hall who has formalised the way audiences respond to the media in terms of positioning: the representations underlying media texts encourage audiences and users to take up particular points of view, particular 'positions'. Not all audiences, of course, adopt those points of view and some only partly agree with them (what Hall called preferred, oppositional and negotiated 'readings' of media texts). What Hall (amongst others) importantly introduced was the way the media can be interpreted by different audiences in different ways – in ways which reflect their social and cultural backgrounds. This seems to us a very important idea – that not everybody interprets the media in the same way and there is therefore not one single meaning to any media text but rather a number of different ways a text can be interpreted or used by audiences.

Having concentrated on media texts and the way audiences and users interpret them, the second section of the book adds the industry context. You will therefore progress from the focus on texts and their audiences and users to considering the role of industries in affecting the nature of those texts. Writers have concentrated on five selected industries: television, computer games, film, magazines and advertising. Each writer has started by looking at a contrasting range of media texts and has then raised questions about what those texts suggest about the industries which produce and distribute them as well as what they suggest about their audiences. Obviously in a book it is impossible to cover everything so the writers have tried to provide you with what they consider to be important areas and a good starting point from which you will be able to develop yourselves through further research. Consequently, the writers have indicated further reference points, including important magazines, books and relevant DVD sources to help you.

The relationship between studying and creating media is an important one. Your study will clearly be reinforced by creating a product and the creating of product is informed by study and research. Creative work is such an important part of all approaches to the media and so the third part of this book focuses on research and creating and evaluating. Here the writers have tried to give practical advice on some of aspects of planning for and creating media products as well as reinforcing, in a similarly practical way, some of the research methods which might help you develop a more informed approach to your work.

You might like to approach any creative work in two stages: the first stage is where you aim to become technically proficient in the medium you have chosen to work in and where you need to do some research into the kinds of products you are aiming to produce. The second stage, leading perhaps to a more informed approach to media production, involves investigating aspects of the media (text, industry and audiences) which will then lead to a more informed media product.

Concepts, ideas, theories and the theoretical

This book is clearly informed by a conceptual approach to studying the media and much of the book's emphasis is on exploring the texts of the media. All writers refer to some common theoretical issues and theories underlying Media Studies but most writers suggest that an understanding of the issues underlying theoretical perspectives is more important than a simple reproduction of them. Certainly, we would like to encourage a critical approach to theoretical perspectives – asking how valid they are, what thinking underlies them and how they can be seen in the context of studying the contemporary media – but we equally seek to avoid the mindless recitation of theory for its own sake. Hopefully this book will encourage you to become critical, independent audiences and users.

Need more?

Some of the information in *Exploring the Media* also features on a web site hosted by WJEC, which includes additional material on such topics as radio, newspapers and the music industry. You can access this information via www.wjec.co.uk/gcemedia

Acknowledgements

It goes without saying that I should thank all those who have contributed to this book. They have all been very generous with their time and approached all aspects of the work with humour and good grace.

I would also like the thank Jeremy Points for his endless support and advice and John Atkinson at Auteur for never doubting we could manage it!

Barbara Connell

July 2008

APPROACHING THE MEDIA

Genre and Narrative

Christine Bell

In this section

- What do we mean by genre?

- Using generic conventions to analyse texts.

- Understanding sub-genres and hybrids.

KEY TERMS TOOLKIT

Genre – the word genre derives from French and means 'type' or 'kind'. In a study of media texts it is used to divide texts into easily identifiable categories. It is a way of classifying media products according to the elements that they share.

Genre Conventions – these are the repertoire of elements that texts belonging to the same genre have in common. They are the aspects that an audience expect to see in a specific media text. They help audiences to recognise the genre and have been built up over a period of time so that they are easily recognisable. For example, a presenter directly addressing the audience is a generic convention of a news broadcast.

Hybrid / sub-genre – a text that combines or subverts the conventions of an existing genre to create a new one. For example, the reality television genre combines, in some cases, aspects of the documentary and game show genres.

Introduction

Genre analysis is often centred on the areas of media and television, but all media texts can be categorised according to their key features including magazines, computer games and radio programmes. Genre, however, is not purely a term created to help media studies students to analyse texts; establishing the genre of a text is also essential to the media industry and to the producers of media texts. Genre is inextricably linked also to industry and audience, key concepts related to a study of the media in all its forms. Clearly establishing the genre of a media text allows producers to attract audiences to products. Audiences recognise the features of a genre and are attracted through recognition, repetition of conventions and therefore expectation of what is to come. Audiences feel comfortable when they know what to expect and return often for 'more of the same'. A good example is the film industry where films tend to establish the genre clearly to attract audiences through familiarity and recognition. The genre of the film is made clear in marketing material including posters and trailers. It is also the case that actors become associated with certain genres, e.g. Harrison Ford with action films or Hugh Grant with romantic comedies. The mere inclusion of the actor's name in the publicity material will signify to an audience what to expect from the film. The audience's enjoyment of a text is further enhanced by recognising key conventions of a particular genre, allowing them to predict narrative outcomes and to anticipate how characters will react and behave in certain situations. Audiences will accept that a character suddenly bursts into song as they understand this is a convention of the musical. This also explains the reliance of the television and film industries on sequels and spin-offs – these are often guaranteed successes because the producers replicate pre-existing successful formulas already endorsed by audiences:

> 'Genres are good for media industries because their potential audience, and consequently their potential profit, can easily be assessed. (Bell, A. Joyce, M. Rivers. D (2005) Advanced Level Media).

However, it must also be understood that genres are fluid and changing, and adapt to changes in society and audiences. Producers are also always looking for new formulas and adapting existing ones in order to continue to attract audiences and to re-invent themselves for new generations of viewers, readers and users. Hence, the advent in recent years of hybrid genres like the docu-soap and reality television formats and the establishment of the conventions of new media including computer games and web pages.

In television, the scheduling of particular genres is also very important in attracting and maintaining audiences.

Zoning – the placing together of programmes of the same genre to encourage audiences to stay watching that channel, e.g. Channel 4 comedy programmes on a Friday evening, or Channel 5 crime dramas *NCIS*, *Law and Order: Special Victims Unit*, *Law and Order: Criminal Intent*.

Stripping – placing programmes at the same time every evening so that audiences get used to watching them as part of their evening's viewing, e.g. *Coronation Street* 7.30pm and *EastEnders* at 8.00pm.

TASK

Look at a scheduling guide for a week's television viewing. Look at the descriptions of the programmes – can you establish the genre of the programme from the description? How does the description of the programme establish the genre for the audience? Find specific examples.

- What can you discover about the scheduling time of particular genres? For example, which genres tend to appear on daytime television?

- Which genres have regular 'slots'?

- Can you come to any conclusions about the popularity of certain genres for particular channels or for specific days?

- Can you find any evidence of zoning or stripping?

- Are there channels that devote air time to specific genres?

This same task can be repeated with a film guide from a newspaper or magazine where the genre of the film is clearly established through the brief synopsis of the narrative, the description of the characters or the billing of specific stars.

Genre Conventions

We have already established that genre conventions are the common features of media texts that situate them in a particular genre. Although we have focused upon texts related to TV and film, all media texts are constructed using recognisable conventions.

TASK

Look at a magazine of any genre. What is there that you would expect to see as a reader of this text, for example, a problem page in a teen mag? Are these conventions common to other examples of magazines belonging to this genre?

Genre conventions can be grouped under the following headings:

- Characters.
- Narrative events.
- Iconography.
- Setting.
- Technical and audio codes.

Characters

Certain characters become associated, through repetition, with a specific genre. Their appearance advances the narrative because the audience recognises them and as a result has expectations about their behaviour and the narratives they may be involved in. Some of these characters may be types or 'stereotypes'. Stereotypes are established through repetition and are linked to the ways in which specific audiences respond to them. However, it is also true that certain genres rely on using stereotypes as a quick way of communicating information.

What expectations would an audience have of these characters?

TASK

Complete the table below suggesting other characters you would expect to see in the genre. Consider their function and how audiences may respond to them:

GENRE	CHARACTERS	FUNCTION / RESPONSE
Soap opera	rebellious teenager	to broaden the target audience
Hospital drama	arrogant senior consultant	to create conflict
Teenage magazine	flawless model	to create aspiration in audience
Radio music programme	'posse' in zoo format	to suggest informality
Computer games	villain	to be overcome/ eliminated

What conclusions can you draw from the table?

- Do certain genres use character types more regularly?

- Are there any examples of positive stereotyping?

- How does the way in which the genre presents the character effect how audiences respond to them?

Narrative events

These are the plot situations that an audience will expect to see in a particular genre. Again, the audience will be familiar with the structure of the plot and will anticipate events and situations that will occur within the overall narrative. Each of these then become a convention associated with the genre. Narrative events do not only occur in fictional texts – the location report in a news broadcast is a narrative convention of that genre, where the narrative is related to order and selection rather than plot. An audience will recognise the convention and be aware of its purpose in giving more immediate and 'on the spot' information about a news story. The same is true of the action replay in a football match, where audiences expect that they will be given the chance to see action from a range of different viewpoints.

In fictional texts specific genres have their own predictable narrative events including: the confrontation with the criminal in a police drama; a family argument in a soap opera; and the amorous misunderstanding in a romantic comedy. The audience have a sense of satisfaction when these events occur, as they confirm its understanding of the genre and its expectations of what will happen.

Texts such as magazines and newspapers have a narrative formula based on order and structure and readers anticipate what will appear in certain sections of the text – this too is a narrative event and readers are comfortable knowing where specific sections are to be found (e.g. in a broadsheet newspaper, world news tends to follow domestic news).

Iconography

This genre convention is related to the objects, costumes and backgrounds associated with a particular genre. These can help to define the genre and to raise an audience's expectations. The iconography of a genre is subject to sociological change as audiences expect more accurate and specific detail. Take, for example, the genre of the hospital drama. Now, in programmes like *Casualty* and *ER*, we see a range of technical equipment and understand its purpose and function. We also see it in use and audiences witness explicit views of injuries and operations involving blood and body parts and relevant surgical procedures. We, as audiences, are surrounded by the iconography of the emergency room and become involved in the action that takes place. Relatively new genres have established their own iconography – for example, gaming and computer magazines have an iconography that includes graphic representations and recognisable logos, designs and backgrounds related to particular games. This iconography often excludes audiences who are unfamiliar with the genre and establishes exclusivity among users.

In programmes set in another time the iconography is used to establish realism. The attention to detail in the backgrounds and props in *Life on Mars* (2006–7) and *Ashes to Ashes* (2008) helped to establish these programmes securely in the 1970s and 1980s respectively – this realism mainly relied on simple props and the audience recognition of them, for example, contemporary police cars and walkie-talkies.

Costume and clothing are also important in establishing genre and help producers of texts to communicate information quickly and effectively to audiences and to advance the narrative. In a hospital drama a character in a white coat wearing a stethoscope has a clear function that needs little explanation as does the hierarchical distinction of the consultant in the suit. Audiences anticipate the role and behaviour of characters according to the clothing that they wear. Clothing can signify social standing, profession, income and values. It can also suggest conflicts within the narrative.

Props and objects can give information about cultural differences – the prevalence of guns and other weapons in American crime films is very different from those set in Britain.

TASK

Study the **opening sequences** of *The Bill* and *CSI*:

- How is iconography used to establish the genre?
- How is iconography used to highlight the cultural differences in the two programmes?

Mise-en-scène
– this French
phrase literally
means 'put-
in-the-scene'
and refers to
everything
that can be
seen in the
shot including
characters,
lighting,
iconography.

Setting

This is a further generic convention closely related to narrative events and characters, and can be genre and text specific. As with other conventions its link to genre is established through repetition which enables audiences to recognise settings and relate them to specific genres and programmes. The tracking shot through the Everglades in *CSI: Miami* is a feature of the opening credits and prepares the audience for the programme that follows. In soap operas characters are inextricably linked to setting in terms of areas of a specific country or individual streets and houses. The characters' houses are seen to be such an integral part of the audience's involvement with the programmes that the producers of *Emmerdale* and the late *Brookside* filmed in real locations specifically built for the programme. Take the characters out of the *mise-en-scène* and audiences would still recognise their domestic setting.

In genres like police dramas, audiences expect to see urban settings with related iconography, which enhances the gritty realism created by producers of the texts. Directors often return to establishing shots of setting during the programme to remind audience where the next scene is to take place, an example being the front of the Queen Vic pub in *EastEnders*.

In non-fictional texts like news programmes, audiences become accustomed to location reports where the setting as a backdrop is clearly established. The Political Editor for the BBC is conventionally filmed in front of either the Houses of Parliament or Number 10 Downing Street. This gives the impression of being at the heart of what is happening and therefore communicating up-to-the minute news.

Technical codes

The way in which a text is filmed / edited and constructed, whether it be moving image or print, communicates information to audiences regarding the genre. The producers of the text will also follow certain codes of layout, design and editing that allow audiences to recognise the form and style of its particular genre. This is established through the repetition of the format – audiences become familiar with this and have expectations of the text. The technical codes of a text also suggest the production values of that text. A 'high concept' action movie is recognisable through the filming and editing conventions it employs.

What is meant by technical codes and how do they relate to a study of genre?

Technical codes can be divided into the following areas:

1. **Camera shots** – including extreme close-ups, long shots and establishing shots.

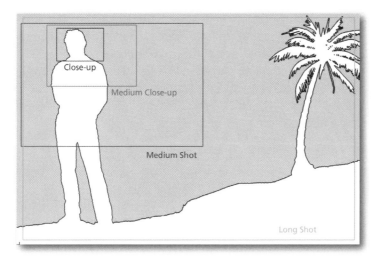

Tracking / reverse-tracking shot – the movement of the camera using a dolly or a steadicam to allow it to smoothly follow a character or the action. In a reverse track the camera moves backwards and the character / action moves smoothly towards the audience.

Certain shots are characteristic of specific genres. For example, in a tense thriller, close-up shots will be used to build tension and to involve the audience. At emotional moments in soap operas the camera will zoom in to focus on a character's face for maximum impact. However, in wildlife programmes in addition to close-ups we expect to see long shots of setting to give more information about where the filming is taking place. Point-of-view (POV) shots are used in computer games where the first-person POV shot encourages users to play as if they themselves are part of the game. Through the POV shot, the user remains in control of the actions of the character as they move through the game. The player *becomes* the character. In the third-person POV shot in gaming, the player controls a character but does not become them:

> 'the third-person point of view allows far greater freedom to tell a more traditional story. This is because the character on the screen is a separate entity and is dissociated from the player. This allows the designer to give characters their own personality and control how they behave.' (Stewart et al., (2001) Media & Meaning BFI p. 126-127)

Third-person POV

POV

Diegetic sound – this refers to natural sound that is part of the *mise-en-scène* or 'sound you can see'. For example, the explosive sound as a gun is fired or the ambient sound of chatter and music in a restaurant scene. Non-diegetic sound is sound which is super-imposed upon the *mise-en-scène* or 'sound you can't see'. This may include the use of a voice-over and music to establish a mood of tension or romance.

2. Camera angles – including high angle, low angle and aerial shot. The aerial shot of the doctors around the hospital trolley became a generic filming convention of the hospital drama *ER*. The repetition of this convention encouraged audiences to suspend their disbelief at being placed in this position. It also allowed them to feel more involved in the action. This same programme makes regular use of the tracking and reverse-tracking shot, again to establish audience involvement and to heighten the pace of the action.

3. Editing – the way in which a text is actually constructed and put together can itself be an indicator of the text's genre. The fast-paced car chase of an action film is a generic convention constructed to convey pace and dramatic action. The editing in the print format of teenage magazines is predictable and has a recognisable format with cover and sell lines placed around a central, usually close-up, image. This image will be brightly lit and airbrushed to suggest beauty and perfection. The front cover will be 'busy' and colourful, and there will be a mixture of font styles and upper and lower case lettering to attract the eye of the intended consumer.

Audio codes

There is an expectation that certain audio codes will appear in specific genres:

- Sound effects – in action films we expect to hear explosions, gun fire, the screeching of tyres. The beeping of heart monitors and other ambient sounds may be conventions of a hospital drama.

- Non-diegetic sound may include a voice-over in a documentary and mood music in a romantic film. Canned laughter is a generic convention of a situation comedy and serves to point the audience towards the humour in the narrative.

- Diegetic sound can refer to the style of the dialogue an audience will expect to hear in a particular genre. For example, a conversation in a heist movie like *Ocean's Thirteen* (2007) will include specific language related to the planning of the crime. In a hospital drama audiences become accustomed to technical language related to hospital procedures. The use of this specific language helps to establish realism.

Music is an effective indicator of genre. The music that accompanies the opening credits to *Match of the Day* or *EastEnders* has become familiar to audiences through repetition and for many people 'says' football and soap opera respectively. Music can be a clue to imminent action. The sound code in *Jaws* (1975) is recognisable to a range of audiences across generations. Contrapuntal music suggests action before there are any other clues on the screen and prepares the audience for what is to come.

TASK

- Listen to the opening sequence of a film without looking at the screen.

- Write down what you think is happening using the audio codes you have heard, for example, sound effects, dialogue, music, etc.

- Watch the film and listen to the soundtrack.

- Watch the opening sequence of another film without listening to the sound.

- Make suggestions for possible music, sound effects, dialogue, etc.

How important are the audio codes to the understanding of the film?

Problems with Genre – hybrids and sub-genres

We have talked at length about genres and how they are categorised and recognised through the repetition of a repertoire of shared elements. However, it is also true to say that some texts are more complex and difficult to categorise because they incorporate the conventions of more than one genre. When we consider the concept of genre from the industry and producers' perspective it is important to remember that here it is not being utilised as a tool for analysis – producers of media texts are constantly looking for new formats or to manipulate existing formats in order to maintain and attract audiences. These mutations are also closely related to how audiences respond to specific genres and their changing expectations linked to social and cultural change. Consider, for example, how the genre of the police drama has evolved from the early days of *Dixon of Dock Green* (1957-1976) through to *The Sweeney* (1975-1978), to the soap opera style of *The Bill* (1984-) and now to the fantasy hybrid format of *Life on Mars* (2006-2007) and *Ashes to Ashes* (2008-).

In the genre of documentary there has been a movement away from traditional informative documentaries to documentaries dealing with more 'popular' subject matter, to those exploiting the format through investigative reporting as in *MacIntyre Investigates* (2002) to the advent of the hybrid 'docu-soap'. This also then has links to the relatively new genre of reality TV, which combines conventions of documentary and game show whilst purporting to represent 'reality':

> 'It was presented in a way that the editors made the show. They had the capacity to make anyone look very good or very bad at the flick of a switch. One of the problems with the whole show was that the public thought it was real. They lost sight it was a game show and it became very personal to everyone watching it.' (Nick Bateman, 'Nasty Nick' contestant in the first British *Big Brother* house speaking on *Panorama* 'Life on TV' BBC1 12th Nov 2000)

TASK

- Watch an extract from a reality TV programme, such as *Big Brother*, and an extract from a more conventional documentary.

- Consider how 'truth' and 'reality' are created through generic conventions – for example, characters, iconography, narrative events, etc.

What conventions of other genres are recognisable in these texts?

It is also interesting to consider the texts that parody existing genres. To create a successful parody, the basic conventions of the text must be clear and understood in order for them to be subverted.

TASK

Study a text that parodies an existing genre, e.g. *The Office* (2001-2003) or *Phoenix Nights* (2001-2002) or similar examples in film, e.g. *Scary Movie* (2000). What conventions of the pre-existing format are used to parodic effect in the new text?

SUMMARY TASK

Watch the opening sequences of texts from three different genres including a hybrid genre. Use the following headings to analyse how the opening establishes the genre:

- Characters.

- Iconography.

- Narrative events.

- Setting.

- Technical and audio codes.

Narrative

In this Section

- What do we mean by narrative?
- How narratives are constructed.

Narrative is a key concept employed to analyse a range of media texts – print and moving image, fiction and non-fiction. However, what we understand by narrative is going through a process of transition as textual formats and audience responses change. Many texts now include audience involvement in the narrative – in computer games the player takes charge and makes decisions about where the narrative will progress. In sports programmes on television the viewer can select the desired narrative which will have a different outcome from the choice made by someone viewing the same text, by using interactive features such as the Red Button.

All media texts have narratives – fictional texts are concerned with a story and a series of plot events while in non-fiction texts the narrative can be analysed in terms of order, construction and genre conventions.

> ## TASK
>
> Storyboard a sequence of 6–8 shots you would use to make a short film of your day so far. Then consider:
>
> - What you have selected and why.
> - What you have omitted.
> - Whether your 'story' is linear or moves about in time.
> - What camera shots you have used and why.

What is essential is an understanding of how narratives are 'told' or 'shown' to an audience – what is omitted is as important as what is included. Non-fictional texts also have a narrative structure – a news programme is constructed to a clear and recognisable format starting with the headlines and ending with the weather. The same is true of a newspaper where audiences know what to expect in each section of the text and on the front and back pages.

Tzvetan Todorov was a Bulgarian theorist who published work relevant to a study of media texts. He suggested that the primary function of the narrative was to solve a problem and that characters pass through a series of stages of a linear narrative where events follow in chronological order.

Roland Barthes (1915–80) was a French writer who continues to influence the study of the ways in which meanings are produced by texts through signs and code systems (semiotics).

Narrative structures

It is important to consider and apply traditional theories before we consider how they may have evolved and changed. Traditional theory as suggested by Tzvetan Todorov (see sidebar, pg. 25) suggests two narrative structures to be found in texts: linear and circular. These theories are important as they give a framework for analysing texts and for understanding the ways in which narratives are communicated to audiences. Todorov allows us to consider the structure of the narrative and how it is moved along through a series of events from beginning to end, while Vladimir Propp (see sidebar, pg. 29) considers the relevance of characters and their actions and responses within the narrative. Roland Barthes (see sidebar), through an understanding of semiotics, equips us with the specific language to allow a detailed study of all aspects of the text. However, not all theories can be usefully applied to all texts and it is important to only use the most relevant one for the specific text to be analysed.

Todorov stated that narratives are led by events in a cause and effect format and suggested the following structure:

The narrative starts with equilibrium.

↓

An action / character disrupts the equilibrium.

↓

A quest to restore the equilibrium ensues.

↓

The narrative moves to a confrontation / climax.

↓

Resolution / equilibrium is restored.

This is a simple structure into which some texts will fit easily. However, we should already be considering the problem posed by the idea of a 'return to equilibrium' or the notion of a 'resolution'. Some texts that seek to challenge audiences offer open-ended narratives leaving the audience to interpret what they understand by the ending. Other resolutions are far from a 'return to equilibrium', for example, the ending of the crime film Se7en (1995) which is bleak and desolate. In this text the audience eventually realises that the only resolution will be a tragic one and there will be no 'return to equilibrium' for the main characters.

TASK

Choose a film or television programme (this need not be a fictional text) that fits Todorov's frame for a linear narrative. Break down the narrative into the structure suggested above.

What experiences do linear narratives offer audiences?

Suggest a linear plot outline for a new film / television programme using these stages.

However, not all texts conform to a linear structure. A key aspect of narrative is its ability to manipulate time and space and to involve the audience at an interactive level with the text. Many narratives are circular in their structure and move around within a timeframe. In films like *Memento* (2000), *Pulp Fiction* (1994) and *Eternal Sunshine of the Spotless Mind* (2004), the narrative is complicated and the audience challenged, due to the narrative structure. In crime drama the narrative may start in the middle, work back to the crime and then forward to the resolution. Split-screen narrative is used where the screen is split into two or three panels with a different narrative going on in each – the audience is more challenged in their viewing as they are asked to interpret what they are seeing at a more complex level through parallel narratives. As regards non-fiction, in sports programmes we readily accept action replays and seeing the same event from a range of different camera angles, perhaps evoking different audience responses.

A study of the narrative of computer games raises some interesting questions. Some narratives are very simple because the world and the setting are more important than the plot. Some games conform to the three-part structure of 'equilibrium – disruption – return to equilibrium', and other games experiment with more complex narrative structures, where there are a series of levels and movement through the levels is the domain of the player. Resolution may never be attained if certain narrative stages are not completed. There may be choices to be made which takes the narrative in different directions and therefore the narrative flow is not constant as it is related to the ability of the player to solve the puzzles. A player may also revisit the same narrative event several times and make different choices leading to different progressions through the game. This interactive nature of the narrative is a relatively new concept for analysis:

> **The way that Lara Croft acts when one person plays her might vary a great deal from the ways that she moves or acts when another person is at the controls. This is why theories drawn from older media (film or literature, for example) can't fully describe digital games. Games also complicate old notions about the relationship between authors and readers, because players determine how the "hero" behaves.'** (Burn et al., 2003, p. 110)

> ## TASK
>
> Look at the opening sequence of *Memento* or *Pulp Fiction*.
>
> How does this opening sequence challenge Todorov's suggestion that narratives are linear?

Narrative techniques

As suggested earlier, the work of Barthes continues to be useful to media students analysing narrative. He gives a clear set of codes which enable us to understand how media texts are communicated to and interpreted by audiences.

Barthes suggested that narrative was conveyed in texts through key codes including:

- Enigma codes – these are used by a range of media, both fiction and non-fiction. These codes control the amount of information that is released to the audience in order to make them curious and want to consume more of the text. Information is often undisclosed until further on in the text. Unexplained 'clues' in the form of enigmas are given early in the narrative. This may be a mysterious figure in the opening sequence, the headlines of a news report or the cover lines in a magazine. Trailers for new films and television programmes are an institutional device employing enigmas and designed to tease the audience and subsequently raise expectations.

- Action codes – these codes are a form of shorthand for advancing the narrative. They signal to the audience a narrative event that will take place, for example, the buckling of a gun belt in a Western or the packing of a suitcase.

Audience positioning in narrative

The privileged spectator position

This is where the camera places the audience within a superior position in the narrative. They are shown elements that the characters in the *mise-en-scène* cannot see. For example, a close-up shot shows one character taking a gun out of her bag, which only the audience can see. In sports programmes this is a common narrative convention, where the viewer, through action replay, sees the narrative more than once from a range of viewpoints. The function is to make the audience feel in a more powerful position in the narrative in that they can then discuss what has happened with increased knowledge and perhaps predict what is to follow.

Apparently impossible positions

Here, the camera gives the audience a view of the narrative from an unusual position, for example from the air or from behind a wall. The audience suspends its disbelief if the position increases its involvement in the scene. In the 'shower scene' from the film *Psycho* (1960) the audience witnesses the action in effect from *behind* the wall of the shower. This is effective because it allows the audience to see the victim and builds tension as a shadowy figure appears on the other side of the shower curtain... Similarly, a car chase can be viewed from an aerial tracking shot, which allows audiences to witness the ongoing action from an impossible position.

The Shining

Psycho

Point-of-view shots (POV)

Here the audience sees the action from different points-of-view that will change its perception and involvement in the scene. The camera may show the point of view of the murderer or the victim or move between the two. This will obviously change the audience's positioning and its response. It is often the case that the audience may be placed in an uncomfortable position by the camera, or one that positions the audience from a male or female perspective. POV shots also affect the way in which the audience relates to the characters. POV can also be established through voice-overs where a character's thoughts are communicated to the audience; and direct address to camera in, for example, a news bulletin or documentary.

A flashback

Here the audience is given additional information about the narrative which enhances its understanding. Older media texts will use more contrived techniques to suggest movement back in time, for example, the hands of a clock moving backwards, pages of a calendar turning or misty filming. Today's audiences are assumed to be more sophisticated and able to decode signs in clothing and other iconography. In the film *Atonement* (2007) the narrative moves around in time and challenges the audience's perceptions with very few clues to what is happening.

Characters in narrative

Vladimir Propp, a Russian literary critic and folklorist, was concerned with the relationship between narrative and characters. Through his research, he argued that stories are character-driven and that plots develop around the actions of characters. He looked at characters and their function within the story. He stated that it was possible to group characters and actions into roles and functions which move the story along. He proposed that there were essentially eight character roles and 31 functions. While Propp's theory can be applied with relevance to some media texts, particularly those with narratives akin to folk stories like science fiction, Disney films and fantasy, it is not possible to apply it effectively in its entirety to all texts. However, it is important to be aware of his work and its application, and his notion of character function still has great relevance. His character types include:

- The hero – who has a mission to accomplish or seeks something, he carries the events through the story. However, in modern narratives the hero can be female.

- The villain – who is driven by evil motives and tries to prevent the hero from accomplishing his mission.

- The donor – aids the hero by giving him help, for example, a magical object.

- The dispatcher – sends the hero on a quest.

- The false hero – appears to be good and tries to trick the hero by giving bad advice.

- The helper – a sort of 'sidekick' who helps the hero.

- The princess – a female character who is the stereotypical 'damsel in distress'. She is also, at times, seen as a reward for the hero.

- Her father – rewards the hero, often by giving him his daughter as a 'prize'.

TASK

Think of a narrative where Propp's character functions can be applied and give examples of the character types above.

These roles can also be found in non-fiction texts – tabloid newspapers often make villains out of political leaders, particularly in narratives involving war.

Whether or not Propp is applicable, the function of characters in narratives is a useful focus of analysis. Certain texts have characters in them that we expect to see. This helps the narrative and communicates information as the audience understands their function and can anticipate how they will behave and even the type of narrative events in which they may be involved.

Technical codes in narrative

The camera 'shows' the audience the narrative through a range of camera shots, movements and angles that have been edited into a sequence. The editing process is where important decisions are made about how characters are represented and events told that will affect the response of the audience. Consider how the 24-hour filming of a reality TV programme such as *Big Brother* is edited into a one hour (with advertisement breaks – so really only about 45 minutes) nightly programme and the opportunities offered to the producers to manipulate 'characters' and storylines.

In the same way, the soundtrack is a narrative device that communicates messages about the plot and what is to come. Tense music (often discordant and uncomfortable to listen to) is a signal of a particular narrative, just as 'action' music (fast paced) signals pace and drama in the storyline.

TASK

Watch the opening sequence of *Thelma and Louise* (1991) and then consider how the narrative is conveyed through the use of technical codes, character and audio codes.

TASK

Study extracts from three different texts – for example, a news programme, a web page and a computer game. Analyse the narrative construction using the following headings:

- Structure.

- Techniques.

- Characters.

- Technical and audio codes.

- Audience response.

TASK

Storyboard the opening sequence for a television drama or a film employing the following plot outlines and using a range of narrative devices:

- A murder.

- Establishing a setting.

- Establishing the feelings of a character.

- Creating an atmosphere.

- Creating suspense.

Representations

Christine Bell

In this section

- What is meant by representation?
- The role of selection, construction and anchorage in creating representations.
- How the media uses representations.
- The points of view, messages and values underlying those representations.

KEY TERMS TOOLKIT

Representation – the way in which the media constructs aspects of 'real life', including people, places, events, culture, ethnicity and issues.

Mediation – the process of editing and construction that the media text has been exposed to before it is presented to the audience.

Anchorage – the text, captions or voice-over that accompany a text and 'anchor' its meaning.

When applied to a study of the media, representation is a complex concept through which we attempt to understand how the media constructs its messages and how audiences respond to that construction. The significant question, as dealt with by Wendy Helsby (2005), is whether the media **constructs** or **reflects** aspects of society. Are the media so powerful that they construct situations, opinions and beliefs that audiences accept as 'reality', or do they reflect the inherent opinions and beliefs that already exist?

Introductory Activities – Understanding Representation

Before you start to study the concept of representation in any detail, it is important to examine how we look at things that are around us and how we interpret what we see according to our experiences and pre-conceived expectations.

TASK

Write a 50-word description of yourself.

Ask your friend to write a 50-word description of you.

How do they differ?

These are two different representations of one person. If you had asked your boy / girlfriend or your mum or your grandad to do the same there would have been differences because of their positioning and relationship to the subject matter – in this case, you.

TASK

Take a photograph of yourself surrounded by objects that mean something to you. For example, clothes you like to wear, a CD of your favourite band, a cuddly toy, your iPod. Ask someone to annotate the photograph decoding the messages you have encoded.

Were there any surprises? Did they interpret the codes differently from your intended meaning?

The ways in which representations are understood and interpreted are affected by a range of other factors, including relationships, context and cultural experience.

TASK

BROAD STROKE PORTRAITS

Someone from your class will stand at the front. Draw that person as accurately as you can. When you have done that annotate your drawing thinking about the following visual codes: clothing, gesture and expression.

What you have constructed here is a **representation** of the person. If everyone in the room holds up their drawing you will see how many representations of that person have been constructed in a short space of time.

Compare the annotations – how do they differ? They will change according to the experience of the person constructing the image. They may be affected by how well they know the 'model', if they recognise the fashion brand they are wearing, if they like / recognise the band they have on their T-shirt, etc.

Before considering specific examples of representation in the media it is important to give some thought to what we are looking for and the questions we need to ask about the representations that are presented to us in a range of media texts. [adapted from 'Representation–an Introduction' Stafford BFI, 2001]

TASK

How do representations work in the media?

Look at the collage of images below. They are all 'representations' of gender that you would find in the media:

- Who or what is represented in the images?
- Where would you expect to find these images?
- Have the images been constructed in any way?
- Do any of the images contain a message? For example, what are we expected to think about these people?
- Choose two of the images – what questions would you ask about the texts?

Think about how you have interpreted the images. You will have looked at the images first and described them – this is called DENOTATION. You will then have tried to understand them and the messages they contain – this is the CONNOTATION of the image.

You will also have deconstructed the image using VISUAL CODES. The most common visual codes used to understand what we see are:

- Clothing – the clothing worn tells us something about the person, for example, a uniform, a football shirt, a fashion craze.
- Gesture – body language communicates messages to others, for example, a wave, a salute.
- Expression – facial expressions are rapid communicators of information, for example, a smile, a frown.
- Technique – the way in which the image is presented carries meaning, for example, black and white, soft focus.

Key questions to consider:

1. What kind of world is being *constructed* by the media text?

What you need to know:

- That the world presented *is* constructed.

- That the reality presented by the text is constructed.

- That audiences deconstruct texts according to their knowledge of the world presented to them and their own experience.

- That characters, locations and issues are presented in different ways.

2. How are *stereotypes* used as shorthand to represent certain groups of people?

What you need to know:

- That makers of media texts use audience recognition of types to transmit messages rapidly. Most media texts including films, magazine articles and television programmes have only a short time to establish characters and as a result offer limited representations. This is especially the case with advertisements (see Section 1 on characters).

- Audiences often feel happier when a character stays within the limits of the stereotype because then they feel that they 'got it right'. They feel comfortable that they understand and can predict their behaviour and narrative function.

3. Who is in control of the text? Whose ideas and values are expressed through the representations?

What you need to know:

- Texts are **constructed** and **manipulated** by the producers of the text.

- A process of mediation occurs in the construction of a media text, for example, a news report.

4. How will audiences interpret / decode the representation in the text? At whom is the text aimed?

What you need to know:

- Representation is linked to the cultural experiences of the audience. The cultural competence will be different for different audiences.

- The ability to decode the representation will also be related to situation / race / gender / age.

- It is also affected by the audience relationship with the individual star / event / environment.

5. What ideology / message is contained within the representation?

What you need to know:

- You need to recognise and be aware of the view being presented through the text.

- Particular interests / views of the world may be challenged or promoted.

- Texts may promote, challenge or judge the roles of gender, ethnicity or age.

Construction and Mediation

By now, you will have learned that the 'reality' we see on television screens and read in newspapers is constructed. Every time we watch or read a media text we are not seeing 'reality' but someone else's version of it. We rely upon receiving our information about a range of events from different sources as we cannot actually be there to witness what is happening first hand. However, what we finally see has gone through a process of **mediation**.

KEY TERMS TOOLKIT

Selection – whatever ends up on the screen or in print, a lot more will have been left out. Someone will have made the decision about what will be included and what to omit. Think about how this might affect how the audience feels about what it sees.

Construction – the elements that go to make up the final text will have been constructed in a way that real life is not. When we witness an accident in real life we do not see it from three different camera angles and in slow motion, this is often the way we view an event in a hospital drama. In 'real life' arguments, we do not have the use of close-ups to show emotion – these are used regularly in films and on television to heighten the experience for the audience. What we see when we watch *Big Brother* is a construction of the hours of filming which have been edited often to show a particular viewpoint (whose?) about a storyline or character.

Focus – mediation encourages the audience to focus upon a particular aspect of the text to push us towards making assumptions and to draw conclusions. In a drama the camera may focus upon a particular character. Similarly, our eyes are drawn to the headlines and cover lines in newspapers and magazines.

Learning Point: Media texts are not 'windows on the world'. They present a version of reality.

Anchorage

Images without words are open texts – the connotations of the image are left to the audience and the associations it might make. At this point, the texts can be said to be polysemic in that they can be interpreted in more than one way by different audiences. Once there are words in the form of a caption, a headline or a description, then the text becomes 'closed' and the audience is told the meaning. The decision regarding interpretation has been made for viewers/readers and they are, therefore, less likely to challenge or consider what they see. The anchorage – the words that accompany the image – affects the representation and how the audience responds to it.

TASK

Choose an example of a current news story, for example, a conflict in another country. List the mediation processes before the story arrives on our television screens. You could start with the fact that the camera person makes a decision about what to film. What are the next stages of mediation?

Now consider the following questions:

- Who is in control of the text?

- Whose ideas and values are expressed through the representation of the event?

- In an event such as that described above, how easy would it be for a particular point-of-view to be expressed? How is the audience expected to react?

TASK

Look at the image of a school below.

For this image write two different headlines, captions and opening paragraphs for a news report that will change the way in which an audience views the image. How might different audiences interpret this image differently because of the anchorage?

TASK

Watch a news report with the sound off. Write two contrasting voice-overs to anchor the piece and change the focus of the report.

How have you changed the meaning of the images through the anchorage?

What effect will the different representations you have constructed have upon audiences?

Dominant Ideology

Whose point of view is presented through the text? This follows on from mediation and considers the idea that those who are in positions of power use that position to communicate their opinions and beliefs. These are usually termed as 'opinion leaders' and for the purposes of this study examples could include politicians as represented in the media, newspaper owners and editors and television producers. They present, repeat and reiterate a particular viewpoint that then appears to become the 'norm' for some elements of the audience. A good example is the *Daily Express* and *Daily Mail*'s view of asylum seekers with headlines like:

June 2006 *Daily Express*, 'Foreign Villains Roam Our Streets', August 2001 'Asylum: We're Being Invaded – Leaked Memo Shows We Are Losing Battle on Immigrants', or June 2005 *Daily Mail*, 'Bombers Come to UK as Sons of Asylum Seekers'.

These headlines encourage the audience to make a link between asylum seekers and terrorists or criminals and offer a very negative representation of this group of people. Language is therefore seen to be a very powerful communicator of ideology and as many people have little first-hand experience or knowledge of asylum seekers, they may accept the view given to them by the newspaper they choose to read.

The more these ideas and beliefs appear in various forms in the media, the more they are accepted and therefore become the dominant ideology. One ideology and representation purveyed by current magazines is equating 'thin' with 'beautiful'. The popular magazines continue to use emaciated models as the true idea of what a woman should look like, although this is far from the 'reality' for many women. Other magazines, like *Closer* and *Heat*, produce paparazzi shots of 'celebrity cellulite' and 'bikini disasters' of those women over a size 10! They also castigate thin celebrities one week and then uphold their 'summer bodies' as an ideal the next, thus offering mixed messages to their audiences.

Those in positions of power who control the media messages received by audiences are therefore also in control of how certain groups in society are represented, and indeed, whether other groups are represented at all.

However, ideologies do change as society changes so there is hope for the death of the 'cult of thinness'. In September 2006 Madrid Fashion week banned models with a BMI (body mass index) below 18 in an attempt to address the messages sent out to young people about how they should look. The organisers of London Fashion Week were urged to do the same. Tessa Jowell, the Culture Secretary and the minister behind the 'body image' summit of 2000 which was set up to examine the effect of the fashion industry on young women, stated:

> **'It is, however, an issue of major concern for young girls who feel themselves inferior when compared to the stick thin young women on the catwalk. They all want to look as beautiful as that and see beauty in those terms...we shouldn't for one moment underestimate the power of fashion in shaping the attitude of young girls and their feelings about themselves.'** (*Media Guardian*, 2000)

Helsby gives another pertinent example in discussing the changing reaction to nuclear weapons. In the 1980s, British women protested against the US Cruise missiles based at Greenham Common Airbase. The press regularly portrayed these women as left-wing militant feminists who had abandoned their families in pursuit of this cause:

> 'They were branded as feminists, with all the attendant connotations of being anti-authority and therefore anti-male. They were seen as examples of the hysterical female, much loved by the Victorians.' (Helsby, 2005, p. 10)

Interestingly, however, the dominant ideology today is that countries should not have nuclear missiles and 'banning the bomb' is widely seen to be the sensible course of action. Greenham Common Airbase was closed in 1992.

Learning Point: Media texts can contain a point-of-view that the creators of the text want audiences to accept.

Representations of Gender in Computer Games

TASK

In groups consider two computer games in terms of:

- Gender representations.
- Theme.
- Narrative, including aims, etc.
- User involvement.
- Technical aspects, for example, first / third person viewpoint, special effects.

One of the main criticisms of computer games is that although they are a relatively new media format, they continue to reinforce traditional gender roles where men are seen as powerful and in control and women are there to be rescued, or are viewed as a reward or a sex object. The themes of many games are also overtly male – racing cars, planning military operations or tracking down a target in a dimly-lit intimidating setting. These 'narratives' (often there is no actual narrative construction), usually involve violence and weapons to some degree even if there is also interactivity and thought involved.

TASK

Look at the YouTube Top Ten Video Game Women and listen to the voice-over which explains how they have been chosen (www.youtube.com/watch?v=cbuaOyZYais):

'The ladies had to be hot and empowering – there are no bimbos here. (www.youtube.com/watch?v=cbuaOyZYais)

What representations of women are being suggested here?

At least boys get to see some action with a high level of exciting interactivity. Those games aimed specifically at girls tend to involve interest-based activities or those concerned with fashion design and make-overs. These games reinforce representations of girls as only wanting to look beautiful and be popular. The animated versions of these games involving Barbie and Disney princesses offer physically unreal representations of women in passive roles. Their main concerns are their appearance and their need to find a man of some description; be it Prince Charming or Ken! Events happen to them in the games and they rarely become pro-active themselves.

However, it could equally be argued that any games that encourage girls to engage with computers are acceptable and that some interest-based games have complex narratives and involve skills such as decision-making and have representations of girls as resourceful and active:

> 'Proponents of games designed for girls believe that any activity that encourages a girl to use a computer is a good thing, even if it might serve to reinforce stereotypical roles. Interest in computer games can lead to increased computer proficiency, an interest in well-paid technical careers and a general increase in the use of digital media by women.' (Stewart, et al, 2001) [Query: need page number]

In the *Pippa Funnell* range of games which deal with the theme of running and managing a stable, the narrative is clear – you have inherited a run-down stud farm and must work to make it successful again. The player moves from one stage to the next only when certain tasks are completed successfully. The rewards involve option choices: to acquire extra land, enter a competition or get a new horse. The mode of address is direct and at times Pippa Funnell (a real show jumper) intervenes to give advice and suggest moves. There are elements of enigma and suspense introduced into the storyline and the navigation around the village is complex.

The issue for media students is not only about the representation of women in computer games but also of men, ethnic minorities and portrayal of violence. The main representation of men in computer games is as action heroes. These virtual images, like the ones of women are physically unreal – good looking, well-toned and white. They can fight dragons, drive fast cars and planes, plan a military campaign and never miss their target. The creators of these representations are also making assumptions, not necessarily correct, about what men want to see in computer games – action heroes and half naked women. It is necessary to challenge these assumptions and not fall into the trap of agreeing with the representations on offer.

The representation of violence in the game format is sometimes viewed as worrying because of the direct involvement of the player and the fact that it takes place in a virtual environment. The player is in control of the violence which, in some games, is extreme and unrealistic. When the player blows up somewhere or 'takes out' a target, they do not have to account for their actions. There is no remorse and, more worryingly, there may even be a sense of achievement. In some games violent behaviour is rewarded and is the only way in which the player can move onto the next level and complete the game. This is particularly true of games with less complex narratives whose main theme is violence and action.

The Ambiguity that is Lara Croft

With regard to issues of representation in computer games, it is important to be aware that all games originated from technology that had been used to create projects funded by the military and many computer game innovators were previously employed in roles related to warfare. This in part explains the prevalence of themes related to war and violence in computer games and plot situations involving hunting down and shooting enemies and targets.

The creation of Lara Croft was a major event in terms of the representation of women in this genre but she can be viewed as both a positive and negative role model. She is a stylised representation of a powerful woman existing in a virtual world which had been seen as the domain of the male. She is a postmodern woman who behaves like a man but, in appearance, is unmistakably a woman. She carries weapons and moves and acts like a soldier but is also openly exploited as a sex symbol. She is overtly sexual and her measurements are nothing less than unreal even if they are 'virtual'. It could be said that Lara Croft was designed by men to please men; yet the irony is that she is heralded as an icon symbolising female empowerment and the ability of a woman to prosper and take control in a violent male world:

> **'The image of Lara has been employed in the promotion of female empowerment. Because she is born out of a male fantasy and so clearly caters to male desires, it is ironic that she has also become a poster girl for a new brand of feminism, recognised under the headings "cyberfeminism", "cybergirlzz" and "girrrlpower". Women are supposed to ignore that the image was created neither by them or for them.'** (Herbst in, Action Chicks, (ed. Sherrie A. Inness), Chapter 1, 2004)

Lara is now internationally recognised and has been transposed into film played by a 'real' sex symbol in the form of Angelina Jolie.

In the computer game, Lara Croft is seen as a dominant character. She is often filmed from below suggesting her power over the gamer. Her stance is aggressive with her gun mounted on her hips and wearing a determined and challenging expression. Her code of clothing is sexual and revealing which contrasts with her role, her behaviour and her involvement in overt violence. Her relationship with the gamer is also interesting. Although she is seen as a strong role model for a female, in the game she is viewed in the third person and, as such, is controlled by the gamer who is assumed to be male. The player follows her but controls her actions as she runs, jumps, meets dead ends, shoots at targets, etc. She actually has no control over her role in the narrative and in fact is controlled totally by the gamer which makes her translation into the active, resourceful heroine of the film an interesting one. For the male gamer, her representation is an ideal one – she is sexy, scantily clad, powerful, gun-toting, hyper-real and perfect. He does not have to deal with her imperfections as he would a 'real' woman – and he can control her without challenge!

Learning Point: Representations in media texts often contain polysemic messages that will be interpreted differently by different audiences:

> **'Once the player tires and the game is over, game and female alike conveniently disappear into electronic vapour. Lara offers a sexy identity void of demands and stipulations.'** (Herbst, Inness, Chapter 1, 2004)

This relatively new representation of women who are violent and are seen as indifferent to violence is also viewed as a worrying and unrealistic one.

'In a world ordered by sexual imbalance, pleasure in looking has been split between active/ male and passive/female. The determining male gaze projects its fantasy onto the female figure, which is styled accordingly.' (Laura Mulvey, 'Visual Pleasure and Narrative Cinema', 1975)]

'The Next Generation People Simulator: they're born, they die. What happened between is up to you. Take your Sims from the cradle to the grave through life's greatest moments.' (The 'Sims2' PC game)]

TASK

Study the games covers for *Lara Croft: Tomb Raider* and *Pippa Funnell*. Consider the gender representation created by these covers commenting on:

- Use of images.

- Language.

- Clothing / gesture and iconography.

- Design and layout.

TASK

Create a new female character for a computer game aimed at girls / women. Use the following headings to formulate your ideas:

- Description of appearance.

- Character traits.

- Game genre.

- Role within the narrative.

- Audience response / involvement / interactivity.

- Write a brief report comparing your character to the representations of a female character in an existing game.

The *Sims2* series

There are some interesting games that offer more positive representations of gender through the creation of a game that can appeal to boys and girls. In the *Sims2* series there is no complicated narrative – the objective is to create a family, choose a home and 'live with them'.

The representation of gender and 'race', or ethnicity, is up to the player and not imposed upon them. The first stage is to create your family from a range of options including their name, the colour of their skin and their body shape. You can choose their clothes, which are not all from a fashion show, and you can choose their aspirations. There are certain restrictions in place, which unlike many computer games, aim to keep this one in the realms of reality – you must have an adult with the family (you cannot create a family made up only of children), but the family need not be stereotypically 'nuclear'. The next stage is to choose a place to live that suits the family's needs. This can be aspirational or based in reality. You are given a certain amount of money and if you can't afford it you can't have it! You can earn more money by, as in the real world, getting a job. You can look for this job in the newspaper that is delivered to your house. There is also a moral code implied – your children must go to school or the social worker pays a visit. The choices in this game are therefore life choices and are based in a 'virtual reality'. The viewing and gaming experience are third person and you can choose to follow and be involved with different members of your created family. Other games in the series allow the player to become involved in going to university and setting up their own business. The game is interactive without being violent; it attempts to establish a 'real world' with real option choices and non-stereotypical gender representations and for this reason is popular with both genders.

TASK

Devise ideas for a new computer game with a target audience of both genders. Consider:

- Characters.
- Setting.
- Theme.
- Narrative.
- Representation issues.
- Audience response / involvement.

Produce the publicity material for the game.

Gender in Advertising – selling beauty

The representation of gender in advertising has come a long way to the point where, as David Gauntlett suggests, men and women in adverts are treated equally and there are few overtly sexist stereotypes employed by the producers of advertisements:

> '...which presumably means that advertisers nowadays take their social role relatively seriously, or, to be more precise, have learned that it is not good business to offend any of their customers with sexist stereotypes.' (Gauntlett, 2002, p. 75)

We no longer expect to see the stereotypes of early advertising where the usual representation of a woman was a housewife who was judged by how white her husband's shirts were as she waved him off to the office.

Men, on the other hand, were often placed in the role of the expert or 'the voice of God' giving women information about changing their washing powder and getting their floors clean. The other representation was as macho men with burly friends in adverts for beer and cigarettes. Yet, despite the generally positive improvements in gender representations it was still found recently that:

> 'Women were twice as likely as men to be in commercials for domestic products and men were twice as likely as women to be seen in adverts for non-domestic products.' (Gauntlett, 2002, p. 76)

The postmodern representation of women that audiences expect to see is more likely to be of a confident, successful woman who owns her own car and can give the average man a run for his money – remember the 'Ask before you borrow it' advert for the Nissan Micra car where just retribution is given to the man who presumed to borrow the woman's car. There was also 'It's not make-up. It's ammunition' for Boots 17 cosmetics where women were seen as dominant and in control.

Interestingly, the notion of 'equality' in advertising now extends to the fact that men as well as women use their bodies and looks to sell products to their own and the opposite gender. However, there is a difference. Men still appear natural and advertise fragrances, moisturisers and anti-wrinkle products but women seem to need to do more. They are involved in the selling of self-modification products like make-up which must be used to enhance and change their appearance – it is not enough to be natural, they have to look GOOD too:

> **'One could complain that women are being told that their natural beauty is not enough, and that make-up is required: that is an unequal message, since men aren't expected to go to so much trouble.'** (ibid.)

Adverts create an idealised representation of beauty and perfection that women and now also men are asked to emulate and live up to. Men are shown to be perfect – well-toned, tanned and good-looking – and women have perfectly made-up faces and slender bodies.

This image is further exaggerated by the use of celebrity endorsement where an already beautiful and iconic celebrity is used to endorse the product. Was Scarlett Johanssen not already beautiful before she used *L'Oréal*?

For many women the use of celebrities to sell beauty products means that the attainment of the ideal becomes an even more impossible aspiration. We are persuaded to buy the products because we believe the representation of perfection that we see and suspend our disbelief at the air-brushed face even when the amazing eyelashes of Penelope Cruz are exposed as fake:

> '...the advertising of the beauty industry does go to a lot of effort to persuade women that they really need the latest skin, hair, nail and leg creams (containing the latest ingredients with complex scientific sounding names). And advertising regularly reinforces the desirability of particular physical looks.'
> (Gaunt, 2002, p. 81)

Learning Point: While representations in advertising have developed since the early days, it is still the case that images of perfection are used to sell products to men and women.

Maybe she was born with it?

TASK

Look at a range of adverts for *Maybelline* cosmetics. TV adverts can be easily searched for by product and brand on www.visit4info.com.

Consider the following:

- This is a long-existing brand that has had its own make-over and has been re-invented to appeal to a new audience. How?

The slogan 'Maybe she was born with it. Maybe it's *Maybelline*' repeats the brand name, uses alliteration and is catchy. It is also enigmatic and suggests what *Maybelline* can do for you so that it appears like natural beauty.

The advert usually includes a close up shot of a face. This has been technically manipulated to show perfection. This representation of perfection is directly linked with the product.

The mode of address is direct and challenging and in some adverts is also provocative and therefore appeals to both sexes in different ways. To women it offers empowerment and, to men, it may suggest availability.

There is always a Unique Selling Point (USP) – something that no other product has (apparently) that will make your lashes longer or your lips shinier. The endorser demonstrates the effect of the product with a heightened focus on the key areas like lips, eyes and nails.

There is always iconic representation – the product is always clearly visible and often larger than life so that the buyer will recognise it.

TASK

Look at a range of *L'Oréal* adverts and consider how the representation of celebrity is used to sell the product. Look at the way age is represented by using Jane Fonda, for example.

They're worth it too!

The concept of marketing cosmetics to men is relatively new. In the past the main product to be sold was aftershave and the representation was always of very masculine role models (like boxer Henry Cooper and Brut aftershave). There was also no mention of the word 'fragrance'. Now we have often more androgynous images and the representations have similar qualities to those used in advertising to women – good looks, sex appeal and a good body. These qualities are pushed to the limit in advertising for *Dolce and Gabbana* where sex is quite obviously used to sell and the models are photographed in provocative poses. The images are of glamour and luxury and the mode of address is direct.

The interesting element of this type of advertising is that the products are for men but many of the adverts are aimed at women as well as men and the responses may be different according to the gender. Take, for example, the advert for *L'Oréal Hydra Energetic* anti-fatigue moisturiser.

The slogan is 'He thinks he looks damn good. You think he looks damn tired'. The 'you' in the slogan is clearly the woman seeing this advert which was in a woman's magazine. The model is stereotypically attractive and the average man would be quite happy to look like this. However, the advert suggests that a woman would have a different response and she is implored to 'help him', showing that the advert is targeted at her. However, there are clues that the producers of the advert are also targeting a male audience: the detail of the product includes information – 'non-greasy texture, non-sticky' – to provide reassurance to the male reader; 'apply in the morning and / or evening over the whole face ' is information we assume a woman would not need; and 'use after shaving – to help sooth razor burn' is directly addressed to the male.

The logo is also interesting. In that the supposed effects of the cream are represented as a re-charged battery – the analogies made are masculine as are the graphics and fonts. This is matched by the square, non-intimidating bottle shape and packaging and the fact that *L'Oréal* gives itself the title 'men expert'. This advert effectively demonstrates how one advert can be encoded to appeal to more than just one audience.

TASK

Look at a range of adverts for men's cosmetics and fragrances:

- What representations of men are used to sell the product?
- Who are the target audience and how are they attracted to the product?
- Is there a second audience who are addressed by the advertisement?

The Dove Campaign for Real Beauty

new Dove Firming.
As tested on real curves.

Dove
Firming Range

This campaign was launched by the makers of *Dove* cosmetics to attempt to raise awareness about what we now accept as normal images of men and women used by the cosmetics industry. They conducted a survey that came up with some startling, but not entirely surprising results:

'**97% of girls aged 15–17 globally believe that changing some aspects of themselves would make them feel better.**' (www.dove.co.uk)

Dove has tried in its campaign to 'go beyond stereotypes' and to produce adverts using ordinary women of a normal shape and appearance and of a range of ages. These 'normal' representations included women with grey hair, with freckles and with curves:

'**The interesting thing here is the risky bet *Dove* is making. Beauty-product marketing has almost always been aspirational:** *I wish I could look like her... perhaps if I buy this lip gloss, I will!* **But *Dove* takes a wildly different approach:** *that chick in the ad sort of looks like me, and yet she seems really happy and confident... perhaps if I buy this Dove Firming Cream, I'll stop hating myself!*' (www.slate.com, 'When Tush Comes to *Dove* – Real women. Real curves. Really smart ad campaign by Seth Stevenson')

TASK

☐ ugly spots?
☐ beauty spots?

campaignforrealbeauty.ca 🕊 | *Dove*

Go to the *Dove* website and look more closely at its advertising campaign and its use of images:

• How does its representations differ from other cosmetic companies?

• How does it use representation to sell its product?

• What messages and values does the *Dove* campaign challenge and enforce?

• How may different audiences respond to this campaign?

TASK

Create an advertising campaign for a new product, using representations which challenge the more stereotypical images of beauty in advertising today. Consider the following:

• The name of your product.

• The slogan.

• Images to be used.

Mock up the layout and design of your print advert.

Storyboard a television advert.

Write a brief report justifying your decisions.

Audience Responses

Christine Bell

In this Section

- The ways in which audiences can be described.

- How audiences are constructed by the producers of media texts.

- How audiences are positioned.

- The ways in which different audiences respond to, use and interpret texts.

Our main area of focus is the relationship between the text and audience which is fluent and changing. In this postmodern, media-saturated world it is no longer acceptable to suggest that there is only one way of interpreting a text and only one possible audience response. Audiences are not mass. They are complex and sophisticated in their responses. It is important also to consider the social and cultural experiences that affect audiences' responses to a range of texts. In this section, the initial focus will be on the range of possible responses and not necessarily upon audience theories. However, the analysis of the response may lead to an exploration of relevant audience response theories.

It is important to move away from the idea that the meaning within texts is already embedded and unchanging and that all audiences respond to messages in the same way. Audiences are made up of individuals who bring social and cultural experiences to their interpretation of any text which may alter the messages they receive from the text. Audiences are not unquestioning consumers as has been suggested by theories in the past:

> **'Far from being turned into "zombies", it has grown increasingly clear that audiences are in fact capable of a high degree of self-determination in the nature of the responses that they make to the products offered to them.'**
> (Stewart et al., 2001, p.25)

Audience Positioning

Stuart Hall, in his research (1973), suggested that texts were 'encoded' by the producers of the texts to contain certain meanings related to the social and cultural background of the creator of the text. However, once the reader of the text 'decoded' that text then the meanings intended by the producer may change.

Hall then went on to suggest three main perspectives involved in the way in which an audience responds to a particular text. This involves how the audience is positioned by the text and its subsequent response.

1. Preferred or dominant readings – this is where the audience interprets the text as closely to the way in which the producer of the text intended. If the social and

cultural experience of the reader of the text is close to that of the producer then there is little for the audience to challenge. If you were a nurse you may well agree with the situations and narratives addressed in *Casualty* because they are within your breadth of experience.

2. Negotiated readings – this is where the audience goes through some sort of negotiation with themselves to allow them to accept the way in which the text is presented. You may agree with some elements of the text and disagree with others. This may mean the way in which you are positioned in a film where you are asked to empathise with a character you do not like, yet you are enjoying the film generally. You may need to adjust your viewpoint in order to get the most out of your viewing.

3. Oppositional or resistant readings – this is where the user of the text finds themselves in conflict with the text itself due to their beliefs or experiences. For example, a narrative in a soap opera that views a woman who is having an affair sympathetically will encourage a resistant reading in a person whose culture is against adultery.

Learning Point: Different audiences respond to media texts in different ways for different reasons.

TASK

Consider some further examples of how audiences may engage in dominant, negotiated and oppositional readings of media texts, for example, in a television or film narrative, a recent documentary and a newspaper report.

These perspectives allow you to begin to understand that one text cannot have a static meaning that is communicated in the same way to a mass audience. This concept should also allow us to challenge 'effects' theories that suggest that this is the case including the 'hypodermic needle' response which puts forward the idea that mass audiences are affected in a particular way by the contents of, and messages within, a specific text

What affects the way in which an audience responds to a text?

Different audiences will respond to the same text differently according to:

- Gender – the relationships between the audience and text according to gender are complex. Men and women will respond to certain media texts in different ways. Certain research has shown that women prefer television programmes like soap operas that deal with narratives concerned with relationships and have strong female characters. Men, on the other hand, apparently prefer more factual programmes related to news and current affairs. However, there are obvious problems with such research as it is generalised and the men / women asked may respond in a way they think their questioner expects. It is commonly

Hypodermic needle effect – this is an example of a media effects theory. The suggestion is that the media text 'injects' ideas and opinions into the audience which, we are led to assume, is passive and unquestioning. An example of this theory would be the idea that violent media texts necessarily cause audiences to behave violently.

accepted that men too watch soap operas particularly those like *The Bill*. It is also easy to say that women would respond to 'lads' mags' like *Nuts* and *Zoo* in a disapproving way – but how then to account for the women who send in their photographs to be published in these magazines or on the website?

TASK

Study the front covers of two magazines or two magazine websites. How would men and women respond to both these texts? Consider the following:

- Layout and design.
- The mode of address.
- The 'gaze' of the central image.
- The cover and sell lines.
- Gender representation.

- Situated culture – this concerns how our 'situation' – our daily lives, routines and relationships – can effect how we respond to media texts; where we are and who we are with has an effect upon our media consumption. Watching a film surrounded by friends or family will be a different viewing experience to one where you view a film alone. This response will change again if you are watching the film at home or at the cinema.

- Cultural experience – this is how our culture – our upbringing, experiences and beliefs – affect our response to a text. This also relates to how our understanding and our view of the world are shaped by our media experience. We may have never visited New York but our media consumption of film and television programmes have constructed a view for us. We may never have been in hospital but we feel knowledgeable about a range of medical procedures because our viewing habits include *Holby City* and *ER*.

How texts construct and position audiences

Here we need to take a more complex approach to texts which go beyond basic content analysis. Texts can be said to construct an idea of their viewer / reader. This can be applied to an analysis of magazines where the magazine constructs an idea of *Men's Health* man or *Glamour* woman. Here we can return to the work done on representation and consider the representations constructed by the magazines and the view of the world and related messages that they communicate to readers. Magazines offer discourse.

The discourses of magazines make their topics and subject matter appear normal and make assumptions about the lifestyles and interests of their readers – hence the construction. McDougall (McDougal, J. (2006) The media Teacher's Book) suggests that discourses contained within the pages of *Men's Health* include:

- Quick-fix problem solving.

- New male sensitivity.

- Male superiority / manipulation.

- Get a six-pack in six weeks.

- Male narcissism and society.

- How to look good.

- How to understand your girlfriend's needs.

- If you understand her needs you will get what you want.

Further evidence of the fact that magazines construct audiences can be found by looking at the press packs for magazines where reader profiles are set out. The reader information provided on the *Men's Health* website states:

'Who is the *Men's Health* reader?

1. Late-20's to mid-30's, predominantly ABC1, a performance-driven achiever, self confident, open minded and adventurous.

2. Advanced in his career with the benefits of success translated into spending power.

3. Older and wealthier than the other major UK men's lifestyle magazines with an appreciation of quality and an aesthetic eye.'

In this way it can be seen that the producers of the magazine construct an idea of their audience and the articles in their publication will mirror and attract this 'ideal man'.

Discourse
– 'a way of talking about things within a particular group, culture or society; or a set of ideas within a culture which shapes how we perceive the world. So when I talk about "the discourse of women's magazines", for example, I am referring to the ways in which women's magazines typically talk about women and men and social life, and the assumptions that they commonly deploy.'
(Gauntlett, 2002, p.16)

TASK

In small groups, look at two or three issues of the same magazine in print or on the internet:

- What are the discourses of your magazine?

- What articles / features can you give as examples of these discourses?

- How might different audiences respond to the magazine differently?

TASK

Looking at men in magazines

In small groups, look at two or three issues of a men's magazine. You are trying to discover the representation of gender constructed by the creators of the magazine and to consider audience responses to this creation.

Consider the following questions:

- What does the front cover suggest would be the concerns of the men who read this magazine?

- Look at the front covers of the magazines – how have audiences been positioned by mode of address, colour, use of images?

- Look at the images of men in the magazine – how could you describe them?

- How does the magazine represent men to men?

- How are women represented in the magazine through articles and images? How does this add to the discourse of the magazine?

- How might women respond to the representations in the magazine?

- What kind of world does the magazine create?

- Look at the press pack information for the magazine. How does this relate to the articles and content in the magazine? Does it reinforce the constructed representation?

- Does the magazine's construction relate to reality?

- Who would be the **different** audiences for this magazine?

TASK

Hot Seating

You should now really know your magazine. Be prepared to take on the role of the reader of the magazine and answer questions about yourself. The rest of the group will come up with questions to ask you about your interests, hobbies and lifestyle which you must answer in character as the consumer of the magazine you have been analysing. You will be put in the 'hot seat' and you will have to answer the questions in role using your research into the magazine to help you.

EXTENSION TASK

- Produce a treatment for a new magazine aimed at men.

- Design the mock-up for the front cover of the magazine.

- Produce the ideas for a web page for a reader profile of the magazine.

- Write a brief report demonstrating how your research findings informed the creation of your magazine, how you have attracted your target audience and evaluating what you have produced.

New Audiences – the interactive users

Our focus so far has been upon how different audiences respond to texts and what affects that response. It has been clear that audiences are complex and changing. With the advent of new technologies and formats including computer games and websites, audiences have become interactive users of the media who are in control and active in their choices. In a video / computer game the user can view the action from first- or third-person point-of-view and can make choices about the narrative and the actions of the characters. Often the domain of the male, as discussed earlier in this section, the computer game allows the male ambiguous control over female characters that have been created to be manipulated by him:

> 'The terrain of computer games has become the site of erotic spectacle; in it the virtual heroine, as Mulvey described, plays to the male, holds his gaze, and is utterly and completely in his control.' (Action Chicks, ed. Sherrie A. Inness, 2004)

Some analysts say that games interact with the user on a range of levels because of the immersion in the artificial world created and therefore the messages encoded in the game are more powerful and elicit a more profound response than in other formats that involve the audience. The experience of 'gaming' is therefore a more heightened one.

The Uses and Gratifications theory was developed in 1975 by Blumler and Katz and was an important study into the way in which audiences interacted with texts.

The ideas of autonomy and control can also be applied to the users of internet websites, where there is a wealth of information and experiences at your fingertips. But everyone will use the internet in a different way.

Learning Point: The ways in which audiences are offered opportunities to use texts and become active is changing *how* we analyse audience responses.

TASK

In groups discuss how you use the internet. Consider the following:

- Which websites you use regularly.
- What information / services you get from these sites.
- How much time you spend online.
- The different ways in which you and other members of your family use the internet.
- What does this tell you about the internet and audiences?

The internet and web pages offer good examples of David Gauntlett's idea of the 'pick and mix' audience. Here the audience uses texts –it ignores some aspects of them and choose the aspects that suit it at that time. The next time people play or search they may 'pick and mix' a different menu – the flexibility is there to enable the user of these formats to do this.

Having come around to the concept of using the media to satisfy the needs of the audience at that moment, it may be time to give some consideration to an audience effects theory, 'Uses and Gratifications'. This is one of the more useful theories as it assumes an active (rather than passive) audience and emphasises what the audiences of media texts *do with* them rather than what the media *does to* the audience. However, the theory must be used with reservations as not all audiences have the needs suggested or use the media in this way. Blumler and Katz (1975) disagreed with earlier theories which placed the audience as a passive mass who could be influenced and would act upon messages communicated by the media. The Uses and Gratifications theory suggests that individuals and social groups use texts in different ways and the audience is no longer viewed as passive receiver.

The identified needs of the audience were later refined as:

- Entertainment and diversion – as a form of escape from the pressures of everyday life.
- Personal relationships /social interaction – identification with characters and being able to discuss media texts with others.
- Personal identity – the ability to compare your life with that of characters and situations presented in media texts.

- Information / education – to find out and learn about what is going on in the world.

TASK

Select either a film or a computer game and explain what 'gratifications' different audiences may get out of it.

However, you must consider that this theory can be now viewed as a simplistic way of looking at audiences that have become more diverse and complex as media formats themselves have become more fluid and changing. This theory assumes that the media itself has identified and catered for the needs of the audience when in fact it may well be the case that audiences respond to the texts on offer in this way as there is no other alternative. It may be that audiences have needs that are not being addressed by existing media texts:

> **'In fact many of our "uses" and "pleasures" can be seen to be "making the best" of what is available and putting it to our [the audience's] use, which may be different from the one that the producer intended.'** (Rayner et al., AS Media Studies: The Essential Introduction, 2003, p139)

SUMMARY TASK

Study any two media texts – for example, two web pages, magazines, film trailers or computer games:

1. Analyse them commenting on:

- Visual codes.

- Technical codes.

- Language and mode of address.

2. What representations are evident within the texts?

3. Suggest how different audiences may respond to the texts.

BIBLIOGRAPHY

Books

Rayner. P, Wall. P, Kruger. S (2001), *Media Studies: The Essential Introduction*, Routledge: London

MacDougall, J. (2006), *The Media Teacher's Book*, Hodder Arnold: London

Gauntlett, D. (2002), *Media, Gender and Identity*, Routledge: London

Helsby, W. (2005), *Understanding Representation*, BFI Publishing: London

Inness, S. (2004), *Action Chicks: New I mages of Tough Women In Popular Culture*, Palgrave Macmillan: London

Stewart, C., Lavelle M. Kowaltzke A. (2001), *Media and Meaning, An Introduction*, BFI Publishing: London

Stafford, R., *Representation, An Introduction*, BFI Publishing/In the Picture: London/ Bradford

Websites

www.frey.co.nz

www.slate.co.uk

www.dove.co.uk

www.menshealth.co.uk

MEDIA INDUSTRIES

Television

Colin Dear

To understand a media text fully you should consider how it has been produced, to whom it is targeted and how this audience will respond to it.

The way in which a text is edited and structured reflects the demands of the target audiences; this will then be represented in the marketing for the product. For example, Simon Cowell is represented as a villain in *X Factor* as audiences find the conflict between contestants and the judge entertaining. His persona is then used in tabloid newspapers to create publicity with mainstream audiences who are likely to watch the programme. These tabloid representations of the star feed back into the viewing of the programme as audiences believe they have gained added insight into Cowell's personality and his relationships with the other judges.

As a result of studying a text, its audiences and the industry which produced it, the distinction between these areas may begin to blur. A star persona such as Cowell's is created partly by the text, by its marketing and by the audiences themselves, so such a concept overlaps all three areas of text, industry and audience. That is not to say that dividing your studies into these elements isn't useful, but you should see these elements as a starting point rather than limits or restrictions to which you must adhere.

Choice of programmes

This section will case study three diverse TV programmes: BBC1's *Six O' Clock News*, C4's *skins* and HBO's *The Wire*.

Television comprises a vast number of programmes spread across a multitude of channels, each watched by a smaller audience than ever before. New technology means that many TV viewers no longer only watch television sets; they use their computers to access BBC iPlayer, 4 on demand, Youtube, myspace and BitTorrent, for example, or they buy box sets of series on DVD. Other audiences increasingly reschedule programmes using services such as Sky+. At the same time genres are splintering and merging into an array of sub-genres and hybrids. All of this means that television is a complex, diverse and rapidly changing field of study.

However, there is no point in only learning how TV works in theory. It is much more useful to look at how television works by exploring different programmes and you have a wide choice available to you. Choosing three programmes to study can be daunting, but remember you are not trying to 'sum up' the whole of television with those texts. Rather you are aiming to gain an understanding of how what we watch on television is structured in terms of narrative, genre and representation; of the different ways in which different audiences consume and use TV programmes; and of how an industry works to create and sell these texts.

Most studies of British television begin with developing an understanding of public service broadcasting and the BBC. Ever since television was first broadcast in the

UK, the BBC's principles of informing, educating and entertaining have shaped discussion of what television should be and what should be broadcast. The BBC News output is a good place to start as it has very clear public service obligations which have to be balanced with the need to attract and keep audiences. Comparing contemporary BBC News bulletins with those from the past is a quick way of identifying the extent to which the BBC has changed as a result of both developing new technologies and increased competition, and yet it still strives to fulfil its duties as a public service broadcaster. Indeed, any programme which aims to attract large audiences whilst fulfilling the BBC's remit, such as big-budget documentaries (*Walking with Dinosaurs* (1999), *Blue Planet* (2001)) or dramas (*Bleak House* (2005), *Rome* (2005)), could be similarly useful texts with which to begin your study.

skins is a useful choice of programme as it is broadcast initially on E4, a digital only channel, and then repeated on the free-to-air Channel 4. This scheduling reflects the impact of multi-channel television and increased competition on terrestrial broadcasters who have created subsidiary digital channels to compete with their rivals. As *skins* is broadcast on both channels you can examine the ways in which the programme targets a niche demographic whilst fulfilling aspects of Channel 4's remit including demonstrating innovation and appealing to the tastes and interests of a culturally diverse society (http://www.channel4.com/about4/overview.html). *skins* is also important in terms of channel identity, generating considerable publicity using a mixture of new technology and more traditional methods, such as good old-fashioned controversy. In fact, *skins* is constructed more like a brand, with viewers invited to buy into a lifestyle, rather than simply watch the programme. Exploring this process of brand creation raises interesting issues about both audiences and industry.

To gain an understanding of television as a whole it is a good idea to study a programme broadcast on a digital channel. Small audiences generally entail low budgets so looking at cheaper programmes such as reality formats (*Britain's Next Top Model*, 2005), imports (*Chuck*, 2007) or imported reality shows (*The Dog Whisperer*, 2004) would be effective choices. *The Wire* is relatively cheap to import, however, its high quality makes it unlike most programmes broadcast on multi-channel television. The reason *The Wire* is a useful text to study is that it reflects a number of trends within the TV industry including: America rather than Britain setting benchmarks for quality; the strategy of targeting small but affluent demographics; and the importance of the DVD buying market. Finally, using *The Wire* allows you to explore the reach of multinational corporations alongside the effects of globalisation.

Globalisation – a process where media ownership, production and consumption cross borders thereby enabling one culture to dominate another through the export of media products and, with these products, cultural ideologies.

BBC1 Six O' Clock News

Text

BBC1 *Six O' Clock News* is an hour-long bulletin, scheduled from 18:00 until 19:00 every week night. National news is the focus of the first half hour; then after 18:30, there are regional opt-outs, sport and weather.

News, like any other media text, is a selected and constructed version of reality; events and issues are represented, not shown, to the audience. The processes of selection and construction are influenced by the needs of the target audience and the objectives of the broadcaster.

On 5 March 2008 the headline stories on the *Six O' Clock News* were:

- A parliamentary vote on the EU constitution and Liberal Democrat backbench revolt.

- The sentencing of a man who stabbed a fitness instructor to death.

- An undercover report on childcare.

- Celebrity drug-users criticised as poor role models to young fans.

Of course, that day, there were plenty of other newsworthy events. That evening, for example, Channel 4 News headlines included the military crisis in Venezuela, while ITV1 led with the ongoing conflict in Afghanistan.

So what makes an item newsworthy? Researchers Galtung and Ruge (Allan and Stuart, News Culture: 62–3, 1999) suggested that a value is placed on an event to help determine whether or not it is newsworthy. News values focus on the properties of the events themselves and are typically classified into 'values', which include: threshold (size); negativity (bad news is more interesting than good); and simplification (simple stories which have one interpretation).

However, news values are just one way to look at what makes an event newsworthy. You should also consider other factors, such as:

- The needs of the target audience.

- The channel identity of the broadcaster.

- Balancing seriousness with entertainment.

British politics, murders and court-cases are considered significant and directly relevant to the target audience, and so frequently make headlines. The BBC has a traditional and formal identity so their news will often select political stories as a lead item. The bulletin then needs balancing with the inclusion of human interest stories, such as the childcare report item.

Seriousness is a necessary convention of the news genre. However, television is an entertainment medium, and the news must appeal to audiences. The selection of headlines reflects this opposition: Lib Dem backbench revolt over European constitutions and Amy Winehouse's drug usage. This opposition is also evident in the structure of the programme.

> ### TASK
>
> - Compile a list of the day's news stories using news websites such as BBC, ITV, *The Guardian*, *The Sun*, *The Daily Mail*, CNN and Al Jazeera.
>
> - Select headline stories and place them in order of importance. Compare your choices with those of the BBC. What factors did you consider important in terms of newsworthiness? What do you think were important to the BBC's choice of stories?
>
> - Watch the news on the same evening. How did the BBC's choice of story differ from other channels? What does the BBC's choices tell you about its news values? What stories were ignored by British TV broadcasters? Why do you think these stories were not selected?

Dumbing-down – a term commonly used to criticise programming which avoids intellectually challenging its audience.

The licence fee – a compulsory charge on all households with televisions which generates approximately £3 billion per year to fund the BBC.

The structure of the BBC News

How does the logo represent the values of the BBC News and its role in the world?

Increased competition from multi-channel TV and new media (including the BBC's own website) has led to some news programmes being accused of 'dumbing-down' in an effort to attract audiences; the digital station BBC3 has even reduced the duration of bulletins to 60 seconds. BBC1 has to compete for audiences but given its status and remit BBC *Six O' Clock News* needs to resist this trend, not only because it may receive criticism over its right to the licence fee, but also because BBC television scores highly with audiences in terms of trust. The trustworthiness of the BBC is undoubtedly related to the perceived quality of its news and acts as a USP for its bulletins (http://www.yougov.com/archives/pdf/Trust070427.pdf.). This means that the BBC has to carefully balance traditional news conventions with attempts to make its bulletins accessible and engaging.

Some of the more traditional conventions of the news include:

- Seriousness – headlines are delivered before the credit sequence, creating a sense of the flow of entertainment being interrupted. This interruption is reinforced by the dramatic non-diegetic music and formal mode of address.

- Professionalism – the costumes, props and use of CGI have connotations of efficiency. The lap-top on the desk represents news that is up-to-the minute and signifies a link to a team of journalists at work behind the scenes.

- Time and place – logos, title sequences and studio backdrops denote the time – 6 o'clock, and the place – in this case London. By fixing this information, the news is given connotations of credibility designed to reassure audiences.

- Tempo – the tempo of news programmes has increased in order to give the news a sense of excitement. Individual items cut quickly between presenter, reporter, actuality (footage of events and locations), expert interviews and vox pops. Graphics, photos, music-beds and sound effects are all used, not only to explain stories but also to energise each item. In the US election item the graphics are accompanied by dramatic sound effects and wipes are used in place of straightforward cuts.

- Tabloid news and dumbing-down – the tabloid style story about celebrity drug-use employs sensationalist headlines – 'Amy on Crack' – taken from red-top tabloid newspapers. Exclusive *Sun* footage of Amy Winehouse taking crack cocaine and a number of music videos are included to further entertain audiences.

Human interest stories and modes of address

The news uses a direct and increasingly personal mode of address, for example the item investigating childcare refers to "your children". By personalising stories in this way audiences are more likely to be engaged as they are concerned about the relevance of news stories to their families. This tactic is one effectively used by middle-market newspapers like *The Daily Mail* and *The Daily Express* to appeal to middle-aged, middle-class consumers.

TASK

Analyse an episode of BBC1's *Six O' Clock News*. Pay attention to the following:

- Representation of the presenter.

- The mode of address.

- The use of symbolic, technical and audio codes.

How have they been used to make the programme appear more interesting for viewers?

Audience

The BBC as an institution aims to be objective. However, this is often impossible to fully achieve, so the news aims to provide a balance of political opinions in order to avoid accusations of bias. Being politically neutral means the news is open to interpretation; different audiences will understand it differently.

As you know, according to Stuart Hall, audiences can decode preferred meanings in different ways. Hall's ideas suggest that the audience is not directly affected by the media, for example, it is unlikely that a Liberal Democrat supporter would change their party allegiance on the basis of a single news story, so they would be unlikely to decode the item that occurred on 5 March about the problems within the party as the news bulletin presented it.

However, whilst the BBC news aims to be politically neutral, like all texts it inevitably communicates a preferred meaning. One strategy that the news frequently uses is the use of binary opposition, especially of 'them' versus 'us'. The 5 March bulletin represents criminals as outsiders from society, their identities constructed by CCTV footage, police photos and descriptions from trials. In contrast, victims are represented in home videos and family photos; distressed emergency phone-calls are played and in one case, described as a 'successful and vivacious business woman... with a zest for life'. This kind of representation has an impact on the way in which audiences read the text.

A dominant decoding of the news would be that criminals are an external threat to us, the 'good' members of society. According to McQuail's version of the Uses and Gratifications model (www.aber.ac.uk/media/Documents/short/usegrat.html), this would provide the audience with value reinforcement and helps to explain the popularity of the news: not only does the audience feel secure, because its surveillance needs have been 'gratified', but the coverage also reinforces our common-sense beliefs. This reinforcing of common-sense is further reflected in the item about celebrity drug-users, in which the extent of the influence of stars on audiences is assumed without question. The Uses and Gratifications model is useful in this context because it encourages us to see that audiences may enjoy texts for a variety of reasons, rather than simply the one intended by the producer of the text.

Contextualising the BBC News

To understand British television you need to start with the BBC. When television broadcasting began (1936), the BBC provided Britain's first channel. At this time it was thought (correctly) that television would be a powerful medium and should therefore serve the needs of the nation rather than make money as a private enterprise. To this day, the BBC operates as a **public service broadcaster**, which means it must do more than entertain audiences and generate revenue – it must fulfil a remit.

Its first Director General, John Reith, famously said the BBC should 'inform, educate and entertain'. This continues to be its mission statement, though now all BBC content should be at least one of the following: high-quality, challenging, original, innovative or engaging. The BBC also has a Royal Charter; a specific remit which is renewed every 10 years and it is paid for by the licence fee, a compulsory charge on all households with televisions which generates approximately £3 billion per year. When the Royal Charter is renewed, the cost of the licence fee is also set; therefore the BBC must show that it is fulfilling its remit (see http://www.bbc.co.uk/bbctrust/framework/charter.html for further information).

Royal Charter 2006 (key principles):

- Sustaining citizenship and civil society.

- Promoting education.

- Stimulating creativity.

- Reflecting the identity of the UK's nations, regions and communities.

- Bringing the world to the UK and the UK to the world.

- Building digital Britain.

Justifying the licence fee involves a complex balancing act. The BBC must be popular with viewers; otherwise the audience will not want to pay for something it does not watch frequently. This is why the BBC screens *EastEnders* (1985) four nights a week and broadcasts *Strictly Come Dancing* (2004-) on a Saturday night in the autumn. But if the BBC only broadcast populist formats, then it would no longer be distinctive from commercial TV, so the ideal for the BBC is to broadcast a range of programmes that are both popular and high quality. Dramas such as *Cranford* (2007) or *Bleak House* (2005) and documentaries like *Planet Earth* (2006) fulfil both functions, but these programmes are extremely expensive meaning only a limited number can be produced.

The news is a key programme for the BBC. Regular news bulletins inform, sustain citizenship, reflect the identity of the nations, regions and communities, and bring the world to the UK. News also attracts large audiences reflected in high viewing figures; The *Six O' Clock News* frequently attracts 5 million viewers, or approximately 25% of the available audience share at this time.

Channel 4 / E4 – *skins*

skins is a controversial teen drama which represents the lives of a group of teenage friends. The second series (Feb-April 2008) consists of ten hour-long episodes each focusing on a different character within a group of friends. This section will concentrate on episode five (10TH MARCH 2008) which focused on Chris, a lovable loser who has been deserted by his parents, slept with his psychology teacher and is primarily interested in taking drugs and having a good time. In this episode he is excluded from college, becomes an estate agent and begins a relationship with Jal, which is then jeopardised as he sleeps with his ex-girlfriend.

Narrative

Throughout the programme the audience is positioned with Chris and events are seen from his point-of-view. For example, Tony, a character partially disabled having been run over by a bus, is viewed from Chris' perspective, struggling to swim in armbands.

Narrative models can be a useful tool for understanding the organisation and structure of stories. Labelling characters or stages in a narrative should not, however, be the end in itself, rather you should use the approach to highlight conventional or unconventional features of the story, identifying how the narrative attracts an audience's attention and maintains interest.

Most narratives conform to a basic pattern: an equilibrium is disrupted, then a hero overcomes a series of obstacles to restore happiness and balance, which is achieved at the end of the story. Such a structure is ideologically conservative – it supports the status quo. This is because stories that follow this model tell the audience that conflict and unhappiness are temporary, that individuals can save the world, that good triumphs over evil and that we will live happily ever after. Clearly, this does not always happen in life.

skins does not fully conform to this pattern as each episode begins with a disruption, in this case Chris being expelled from college. However, he does still attempt to repair this disruption and completes his quest. Then, at the point when Chris has everything – the girl, the job, the flat – meaning he has effectively reached a 'happy ending', his life is disrupted once more. Just as expulsion from college was his fault – his crimes denoted in CCTV footage – Chris makes another mistake, and has sex with his ex-girlfriend.

The lives of the characters in *skins* are represented as constantly being disrupted. Consequently the characters conform to stereotypes of youth, causing their own disruptions by acting irresponsibly. Not only does Chris lose his girlfriend, he also loses his job and his home because he moves into one of the flats he is supposed to be letting. This is where we leave Chris at the end of the episode, but it isn't a state of equilibrium as his life is in turmoil. Ideologically the programme challenges the belief that everything will turn out alright in the end, and characters are left facing new conflicts and problems.

Representation

Where *skins* differs from many other teen dramas is that, despite the turmoil and the problems, the programme is also a celebration of youth, each episode featuring scenes set in gigs, clubs and house parties. The characters dress well without conforming to mainstream trends. Their lifestyles are exciting, soundtracked by a mixture of alternative music, and whilst not all the characters conform to the male or female gaze, the way they live and their group of friends make them desirable and aspirational.

The characters' use of drugs is normalised without the characters being demonised. When attempting to sell his first house Chris paints an idealised picture of life in the house, finishing with 'imagine skinning up in the back garden... with the kids'. These customers are surprised rather than shocked, and buy the house.

The narrative of *skins* lacks the binary oppositions conventionally found in teen drama, for example:

- Children vs. parents.
- Youth vs. experience.
- Irresponsibility vs. responsibility.

This absence of these oppositions stems from the representation of the adults, who are as flawed as the young characters: Chris' ex-girlfriend was his teacher; his father and mother desert him; even the college principal is foul-mouthed and expels him because of the college's statistics. Characters are divided into those that are likeable and those that are not, regardless of age. The middle-aged estate agency manager bonds with and supports Chris whereas his young colleague is represented as annoying and aggressive.

It is often claimed that programmes like *skins* are more 'realistic' than other teen programmes such as *Hollyoaks* (1995-) and *The OC*. What those who say

See notes on Mulvey's 'male gaze' theory at: http://www.aber. ac.uk/media/ Documents/gaze/ gaze09.html this mean is that the characters and narratives transcend simple stereotypes and the straightforward clash of opposites. Chris is a complex character; he is simultaneously likeable but cheats on his girlfriend, even while he genuinely wants the relationship to work. These complex representations of characters and their behaviour can be linked to discussions about realism, as this reflects our actual experiences more closely than less-developed and more stereotypical characters.

skins – the audience

The Uses and Gratifications model aims to explain how audiences use the media to fulfil their needs. McQuail (www.aber.ac.uk/media/Documents/short/usegrat.html) explains a number of uses which provide a useful starting point when explaining the appeal of media texts. These can be effectively used to analyse aspects of the audience relationship. Read the summary below and see if you agree:

- Diversion – the audience of teenagers will be entertained by the drama and comedy conventions used in the text.

- Value reinforcement – *skins* represents values such as enjoying life and friendships as an alternative to family which the viewers may share.

- Reality exploration – audiences might relate to Chris' relationship problems, evaluating their own behaviour as a result of viewing.

However, what is important about *skins* is that audiences are encouraged to do much more than simply watch. The programme encourages audiences to use interactive content across a range of media forms. E4's demographic (16–34, predominantly ABC1s) are at the forefront of social networking and downloading content instead of watching television in the traditional sense. They are also quite likely to engage in fandom. *skins* exploits these factors, presenting an active audience with the opportunity to interact with other fans, as well as characters from the show.

E4's *skins* web site allows fans to download exclusive material never broadcast on television, including mini episodes and video blogs featuring the cast in character. The audience is able to gain greater insight into the characters and the direct mode of address encourages a greater sense of connection between character and viewer. This suspension of disbelief is reinforced through the use of profiles and blogs written by each of the characters.

Giving the characters lives outside of the programme (even between series) may allow the audience to gratify its personal relationship needs. Many viewers do use social networking sites such as Myspace, Facebook and Bebo to become part of a wider community, based on, but not limited to, the TV programme. Viewers can become one of *skins'* 140,000 Myspace friends, join official and unofficial Facebook groups, including a 4,000 strong campaign to win a *skins'* party for Leeds.

The internet revolutionised and redefined fandom in the 1990s, enabling fans to communicate with each other, unrestricted by geography. Much attention has been paid to the phenomenon of fan fiction. Fans of *skins* programmes such as *Buffy the Vampire Slayer* (1997–2003) wrote stories, even novels, using TV programmes as source material. *skins* encourages similar, but more technologically focused (and socially acceptable) practises. *skins*' site allows audience members to create their own related projects, including redesigning the series logo, restyling the characters and producing party projections, used as backdrops for *skins* nights. These creative outlets for expression could allow the audience to gratify self-actualisation needs.

Audiences use *skins* as both an inspiration and outlet for their creativity.

TASK

Starting at E4's homepage, explore the interactive content and activities available to fans of *skins*. Use both official and unofficial sites and then assess the interactivity of each text by asking the following questions:

- What can fans of the programme do?
- What is the relationship between the interactive content and the programme?
- Who are the target audiences for the interactive content?
- How does the interactive content gratify the audience needs? (Use McQuail's categories as a starting point but you can adapt them or create your own as well.)

Taking a further step away from the programme, *skins life*, an online magazine devoted to the lifestyle of *skins'* characters was launched by the show's production company, Company Pictures. This site enables users to upload artwork, video material and anything else deemed suitably creative. It also features magazine content focused on style and music, whilst promoting a live tour, which further extends the brand. There is even a competition offering bands or artists the chance to be support acts at these concerts.

Industry

E4 is a digital channel launched by Channel 4 in 2004 to specifically target 16–34 year-olds. This demographic is extremely important to advertisers as it is a group with a high disposable income but who are difficult to reach, as, contrary to popular opinion, they actually watch less TV than other audiences. This makes successfully targeting this audience difficult, but potentially highly profitable.

Channel 4 is a public service broadcaster but, unlike the BBC, is commercially funded. Its remit focuses on the following:

- Innovation.
- Risk-taking.
- Appealing to and representing minorities.
- Engaging young audiences.

E4 was launched as 'Channel 4 without the boring bits' (Kevin Lygo, Channel 4's Director of TV), presumably referring to those programmes not aimed specifically at youth audiences, such as Channel 4 *News and Dispatches*. It has been a relative success, regularly attracting hundreds of thousands of viewers and establishing a youthful channel identity. At the bottom line, it averages more than the 1% of the available audience share demanded by its parent channel.

Yet despite this success, E4 has an identity problem because the channel schedules few of its own programmes and relies heavily on previewing Channel 4 programmes, such as *Hollyoaks* (1995–), *Big Brother* spin-offs (2000–) and repeats of *Friends* (1994–2004). *skins* offers E4 the edgy, distinctive identity the channel needs whilst delivering huge viewing figures: over 800,000 people watched the first episode of series 2.

The extensive marketing campaign made use of print adverts, expensive promos and internet banners. For the second series the cast also appeared widely, from *Friday Night with Jonathan Ross* on BBC1 to the cover of *Attitude* magazine, generating maximum publicity from their newfound celebrity status. Word of mouth has also made a major contribution to the promotion of *skins* partly as the result of its online presence outlined above.

TASK

Analyse this poster for *skins* and consider the following questions:

- How is youth represented?
- Explore the ways in which the poster contributes to E4's channel identity?
- In what ways does the poster appeal to the target audience?

The Wire

This section looks specifically at Episode One of Season Three (2006, UK).

Text

The Wire is a critically acclaimed American crime drama spanning five series. Each series consists of 13 one-hour episodes which follow a wire-tap investigation into drug-dealers in Baltimore. This investigation is the central thread of a sprawling narrative structure, featuring a large ensemble cast, which represents a dystopian America. Whilst never gaining spectacular viewing figures, like many HBO dramas, *The Wire* has a dedicated cult following.

Genre

Genre is best understood as a series of relationships between producers, texts and audiences. In order to keep audiences interested many texts challenge expectations, so you should pay attention to how texts challenge, as well as conform, to conventions. Crime drama in particular is a complex genre consisting of many sub-genres and hybrids and can traditionally be divided into three main sub-genres depending on audience positioning. The audience can be positioned with:

- The detectives.
- The criminals.
- The victims.

In *The Wire*, each of these strands has its own narrative. *The Wire* also uses conventions from various sub-genres and transgresses boundaries of them all, for example:

- Procedural crime dramas (programme examples include *NYPD Blue* (1993-2005) and *Law and Order* (1990)). Although *The Wire* does not focus on a single, specific crime, one investigation – a wire-tap – develops across the five series. This allows the producers to extend the procedural crime drama format to include a surveillance unit, the homicide division and the Assistant State Attorney, as well as the hierarchy of commissioners.

- Gangsters – the lives of criminals are represented. However, these narrative strands do not focus solely on the main criminals as is conventional. *The Wire* also includes narrative strands focusing on junior dealers, and even on Bubbles, a homeless crack-head who is introduced in this episode, trouser-less and attempting to sell scrap-metal.

- Buddy-cop sub-genre (which stems from the American dime novel tradition) –Detectives Ellis and Carver patrol the streets of Baltimore, chase criminals and use violence. This action-based tradition is anchored by the use of the *Shaft* (1971) theme, played by Herc as they chase criminals. However, their violence is represented as brutality through the beating up of children involved in drug dealing, then charging them with loitering.

Narrative

The narrative of *The Wire* appears more complex than that of many other TV programmes. Some key features that contribute to this complexity include:

- No recap of previous episodes.

- Each programme features a pre-credit scene, which does nothing to progress the continuing narratives.

- No crime is committed to disrupt the equilibrium.

Yet, the whole of Episode One of Season Three works to establish a state of equilibrium: the wire-tap team is failing; Jimmy's wife is seeing another man; the Barksdale organisation has lost territory; and Stringer is running the drug-dealing business because Avon is in prison. Rather than representing disruptions this episode constructs enigmas: who is Proposition Joe? How can the police lower crime statistics? Why is the councilman undermining the Mayor? Each event develops the narrative structure, creating new enigmas, disrupting the previous disruptions and giving each character new priorities. Few, if any, of these enigmas are resolved and, consequently, *The Wire* is difficult to analyse using any of the traditional narrative theories.

TASK

Watch an episode of *The Wire* (American, HBO) and a more traditional crime drama like *Waking the Dead* (British, BBC1). Construct a flow chart for each which outlines the main elements of the narrative:

- How do they compare?

- What does this tell you about the complexity of *The Wire*'s narrative?

There is no hero in *The Wire*. Each character has their own quest, although many are not clearly defined or cannot be achieved. In this episode Detective Jimmy McNulty's goal of charging Stringer Bell is not shared by the rest of his unit. It also seems highly unlikely to be achieved given that their surveillance operation is failing. Ellis and Herc have no quest beyond their day to day task of stopping drug-dealing, which they are unable to complete, and the criminals sell drugs with no thought for the future.

However, the central binary opposition of police versus criminals is conventional and does help to structure the programme; yet within both sides there are a number of significant conflicts. The criminals are divided into two gangs with separate territories, and Series Three introduces a new gang led by Marlo. The police are divided according to hierarchy – Majors against the Commissioner, McNulty against Lieutenant Daniels. Each character has their own agenda which places them in opposition with colleagues and superiors. All these conflicts are given the same level of importance, including those that are personal, such as McNulty's jealousy of his ex-wife's new partner. Again, a complex set of relationships are presented to the audience.

The fact that episodes of *The Wire* do not conform to simple narrative models may help to explain why the programme feels so different to other TV crime dramas. Enigmas are rarely resolved, 'heroes' don't complete quests and the narrative is far more open than is conventional for the medium.

Audiences

According to Steven Johnson, 'some narratives force you to do work to make sense of them' (2005, p65). *The Wire* is part of a trend within American drama, which asks audiences to make sense of information that has been deliberately withheld or left obscure. Johnson calls this process 'filling in' and controversially claims that this process is helping make audiences more intelligent, a trend clearly identified in IQ tests.

One of the distinctive features of *The Wire* is that it does require greater activity on the part of the audience than other, more traditional crime dramas. In order to understand *The Wire*, it is necessary for the viewer to follow numerous interconnected narratives involving a huge array of characters; more than 20 in this episode alone. No differentiation is made between returning characters and new faces like Councilman Tommy Carcetti; the audience is expected to pick up the storyline of political conflict without exposition. A single scene may refer to several storylines simultaneously. Audiences are also required to work out much of what is going on for themselves as information important to the plot is frequently withheld. Clearly, different audiences will respond to this text in different ways.

TASK

Select any episode of *The Wire*. List the characters, including information about them such as their occupation, quest and status. Then create a visualisation chart, (a visualisation chart is like a suspect board you will be familiar with from watching television crime dramas. Use sheets of A4 paper with the names of the main characterson. Place on a large sheet of sugar paper - or on a wall - in any configuration and link the characters together, explaining the links between them), identifying the main characters within the episode and highlighting the links between them. Use your map to answer the following questions:

- How many narrative strands does the audience need to follow simultaneously?

- Identify the enigmas in the episode: what questions are raised by these?

- Which questions are left unanswered at the end of the episode?

Richard Dyer (1977) argues that some genre forms are 'utopian' because they allow a kind of fantasy escape.

Dystopia and audience pleasure

Usually, television is aspirational; representing glamorous, exciting worlds where good frequently triumphs over evil in new and dramatic ways. In contrast, *The Wire* depicts society in the bleakest possible terms. Characters are trapped in a decaying city, where crime and violence are rampant. *The Wire* represents Baltimore, and by implication the USA, as a dystopia.

It attempts to be realistic and thought-provoking, offering audiences insight into the decline of an American city, presenting them with complex moral questions and with characters more fully developed than those usually represented on TV. *The Wire* gives viewers an opportunity to experience situations they would never encounter, or wish to, in their real lives and therefore offers a different sort of escapism.

Texts which offer utopian pleasures represent lives which are not subject to the limits and problems experienced by viewers. *The Wire* is the opposite in that the characters' limits and problems are far weightier than those its audience is likely to encounter. Audiences may be able to relate to these features, but at the same time the characters' lives are sufficiently removed from and different to their own, so the audiences are entertained by them.

Utopian texts feature characters in possession of human power, meaning characters' actions can change the states in which they exist, whereas the characters in *The Wire* are pawns controlled by the systems in which they live. Everyone from drug-users, like Bubbles, to police commissioners experience powerlessness, denied the opportunity to take significant action by their roles within hierarchies, bureaucracy, addictions, laws, environments and their own flawed characters.

Monopoly
– where there is
only one provider
for certain goods
or services.

Perhaps more strikingly, there is a complete absence of transparency. Transparency refers to the clear differentiation between right and wrong, good and evil; but in *The Wire*, Stringer appears to be a criminal intent on pacifying the drug wars, whilst the police are corrupt and violent.

Contrasting the programme with Richard Dyer's theory of Utopian Pleasures may help to explain how *The Wire* offers the audience a very different viewing experience. As the representation of dystopia denies the audience fantasy and familiar forms of escapism, *The Wire* is difficult to enjoy in the same ways as other mainstream television programmes. Complex and pessimistic, it is a difficult watch, which may explain its critical acclaim but lack of viewers.

Industry

The Wire is broadcast in Britain on the digital channel FX, which screens high-quality US imports such as *Dexter* and *NCIS* in order to target 25–44 year-old, ABC1 males. Attracting a wealthy niche audience is the main strategy employed by merely digital channels. Sometimes referred to as narrowcasting (rather than BROADcasting) this approach has proved successful, enabling a clear channel identity to be sold to audiences and advertisers.

Fragmented audiences and multi-channel TV

Success for digital channels – often defined as anything over 1% audience share (compared with ITV1's 18%) – is relatively small. FX's biggest ever hit, *Dexter*, topped 300,000 viewers (in comparison, 8 million regularly watch BBC1's *EastEnders*). Given the smaller audience share, digital channels have to survive on limited budgets. This is why multi-channel TV is dominated by cheap television. A certain standard of content is required by advertisers, so some channels exist purely on the money generated by phone-ins. Otherwise, the cheapest programmes to broadcast are repeats and imports. Reality TV can be cheap to produce, but many channels buy in all their programmes. FX is a typical digital channel in that its schedule is made up exclusively of US imports.

What makes FX unusual is the high quality of its imports. This is partly because US television is currently enjoying something of a golden-age. The most significant cause for the increasing number of quality US dramas is the American cable channel HBO, which broadcast *The Sopranos* (1999–2007), *Six Feet Under* (2001–05), *Deadwood* (2004–06) and *The Wire*. The channel is paid for by subscription so programmes are not interrupted by adverts. HBO itself is a comparatively expensive channel to subscribe to, so it broadcasts these complex dramas to appeal to wealthy, highly-educated subscribers. The success of HBO had led to other US networks imitating complicated narratives and darker themes in their programmes. FX is able to acquire these programmes relatively cheaply (certainly much more so than originating them itself), and in doing so create a distinctive channel identity. All channels, including digital channels, need a recognisable identity, especially now that audiences are overwhelmed with choice.

In a monopoly, the market is controlled by one. In an oligopoly, the market is controlled by a select few.

TASK

Create a channel profile for FX and consider how *The Wire* has contributed to this identity.

FX is also able to afford more expensive, quality drama, even showing some first-run series in the UK, because it is part of the Fox network, which is a division of Rupert Murdoch's News Corp. The world's media is dominated by a handful of multinational, converged companies including News Corp and Time Warner, which owns HBO. FX has the advantage of being able to broadcast programmes from the Fox network in the US. BSkyB is also part-owned by News Corp, so FX is distributed via another of Murdoch's companies.

TASK – RESEARCH OWNERSHIP

- Use the internet to find out who owns more of the popular digital channels, including Paramount, Trouble, Bravo, Living and MTV.

- Explore the suggestion that multi-channel TV is becoming an oligopoly.

End Note

Influential TV critic Charlie Brooker has championed *The Wire* in his weekly (26/01/08) *Guardian* column. The newspaper termed the programme '...the greatest TV series you've never seen...', has run numerous articles on the show and, in a world first, offered readers the opportunity to download the first episode, for free, from its website. This publicity has succeeded in raising the public's awareness of the channel and the programme.

TASK

With reference to the *Six O' Clock News*, *skins* and *The Wire*, consider how important individual programmes are to broadcasters. You may wish to refer to:

- Attracting diverse audiences.

- Public service and channel remit obligations.

- Channel identity – scheduling, ratings, advertising and publicity.

- Programme content, representation and identification.

BIBLIOGRAPHY

Internet

The Guardian's online archive

http://www.guardian.co.uk/Archive/0,,,00.html?gusrc=gpd

What's this Channel 4?

http://www.channel4.com/culture/microsites/W/wtc4/

Books

Greber, G. (ed.) (2001), *The Television Genre Book*, BFI: London

Johnson, S. (2005), *Everything Bad Is Good For You*, Penguin: London

Rayner, P., Wall, P. and Kruger, S.Peter (2004), AS Media Studies: The Essential Introduction, 2nd edition, Routledge: London.

Rehahn, E. (2006), *Narrative in Film and TV*, Auteur: Leighton Buzzard

Computer Games

Sam Williams

The computer and video games industry is one of the most rapidly expanding cultural industries. The market is expanding at a dramatic rate: in 2007 software sales reached $9.5 billion, which was 28% up on the previous year (www.Theesa.com). The industry's economic impact is illustrated further through data from the Entertainment Software Association showing that *Halo 3*, the best-selling title of 2007, took in more revenue in its first day of sales than the biggest opening weekend ever for a movie (*Spider-Man 3*, 2007) and the final *Harry Potter* book's first day sales. Games culture has grown rapidly and with nine games sold every second, gaming has become big business.

For many years gamers have had a choice of platforms. From the late 1980s and early 1990s the market was dominated by Nintendo and Sega; in the mid 1990s, Sony and Microsoft emerged as major players. The choice of consoles has also rapidly expanded and gamers can now select from several hand-held and console-based devices such as the Xbox, Playstation, DS, PSP and the so-called next generation systems like the Xbox360, Playstation 3 and Wii. Many games are also played on PCs. Games themselves have become more diverse and complex, and often require users to be active constructors of meaning. According to Newman and Oram, they are 'an important part of an emergent "new media"' (Teaching Video Games, BFI Publications), a new media whose popularity can be attributed to the convergent nature of the media form itself and its ability to utilise other media forms such as magazines, adverts, films and the internet.

Until recently, the study of computer and video games as media forms was one that was largely neglected and perhaps the idea of playing and studying games was seen as something a little 'childish'. However, the average gamer according to the ESA is 33 years-old and has been playing for at least 11 years. Perhaps our notion of computer games and gaming is one that needs addressing and updating?

The growth in the games market means that there is a vast range of games you can choose from to study. This section will consider three texts – *World of Warcraft*, *Tomb Raider* and *Bully* – approaching each one from the areas of text (genre, narrative and representation), audiences / users and industry.

The Entertainment Software Association (ESA) – the US association exclusively dedicated to serving the business and public affairs needs of companies that publish video and computer games for game consoles, personal computers and the internet.

World of Warcraft

Blizzard Entertainment – a division of Vivendi Games, is an American computer game developer and publisher.

MMORPG – A Massively Multiplayer Online Role-Playing Game.

Persistent World – a world that continues to exist and evolve while the player is away from the game. In this sense it is similar to the real world where events continue to happen whether a person is asleep or absent from the action.

CRPG – a Computer Role Playing Game.

Genre and context

The growth in the games market can clearly be seen in the success of *World of Warcraft*. Developed by Blizzard, it was the top-selling computer game of 2006, outselling its competitors *Final Fantasy XI* and *Everquest*. It is currently the world's largest online role-playing game (or MMORPG), and, according to Blizzard has over 10,000,000 monthly subscribers.

World of Warcraft is part of the ever-growing genre of online computer role-playing games in which a large number of players interact with one another in a virtual world. In this fantasy world, players assume the role of a fictional character and take control over many of that character's actions. A player can choose how the character looks, behaves, what they do, what they say and when. MMORPGs are distinguished from single-player or small multi-player CRPGs by the number of players, and by the game's persistent world.

These games were inspired by early role-playing games such as *Dungeons and Dragons* and are structured in similar ways. The central stories usually involve a group of characters (a party) who have joined forces to accomplish a mission or 'quest'. Along the way the adventurers must face a great number of challenges and enemies (usually monsters inspired by fantasy, and, to a lesser extent, science fiction and classic mythology).

Each character has a range of skills, attributes and possessions that a player is able to track on-screen. These include energy levels, skill levels in a particular area, items a character has in his / her bag. These are traditionally displayed to the player on a status screen as a numeric value, instead of a simpler abstract graphical representation such as the bars and meters favoured by other computer games. In this way a player can instantly see how 'healthy' their character is and also when they are about to die!

Note the range of skills, etc. represented on screen.

Who are you? The representation of Self

The use of an avatar is a key feature of the MMORPG and so one of the first decisions you will have to make playing *World of Warcraft* is to choose your character. A player can choose from ten different races living in one of two factions. Will you be 'good' and part of the Alliance or part of the slightly more sinister Horde?

These avatars are, in many ways, similar to the representations people construct via social networking sites like Bebo or Facebook, where a persona is created through the images people choose to upload and the information included in their profiles. (We might consider whether these multi-user social networking sites like these are also MMORPGs?)

In *World of Warcraft* the characteristics and personality traits of each race and class are something to consider before making your choice.

The official *World of Warcraft* strategy guide offers clear advice about choosing your character because the avatar you adopt says something about yourself. According to the guide you should consider whether 'you want to get up close and personal?' or 'Is ranged combat more your style?' or 'Is magic a way of life?' (Official World of Warcraft guide).

There is a clear implication that the game expects that your avatar will be a representation of yourself. You can focus on your personality traits and highlight the aspects of yourself that you choose. In some ways you create your own star image. In *I, Avatar*, Mark Stephen Meadows defines an avatar as 'a social creature

Avatar – a computer user's representation of himself or herself. This could be a three-dimensional character or just a two-dimensional icon or picture.

Class – *World of Warcraft* has nine character classes that a player can choose from. Each class has a set of unique abilities and talents.

Second Life – an internet-based virtual world that was launched in 2003. Residents can interact with one another via avatars in a complex social network.

dancing on the border between fiction and fact' (2008), a kind of online virtual body. Within the fantasy world of *World of Warcraft* this difference may appear to be more obvious, as you are clearly not a Night Elf, Gnome or an Orc. However, it is not always quite this straightforward because in *World of Warcraft* you may stress or change aspects of your personality through your avatar. You could become the warrior that you are not brave enough to be in real life or highlight your intelligence by becoming a warlock or shaman. This can be taken to extremes in other MMORPGs where you can completely recreate yourself. The highly popular and controversial *Second Life* is an alternate world where you can be someone else just by setting foot there. Unlike *World of Warcraft*, in *Second Life* you have complete control over your choices from skin colour to hair style to breast size.

Second Life

TASK

Compare MMORPGs like *World of Warcraft* and *Second Life*. What similarities and differences can you see? Consider the following:

- Genre conventions.

- Narrative structure.

- Representational issues.

- Target audience.

The following sites may be useful:

www.secondlife.com

http://www.guardian.co.uk/technology/secondlife

Part of *World of Warcraft*'s advertising strategy uses the idea of character identification and uses actors Mr T and William Shatner in a recent television advertising campaign to explain their Warcraft avatars.

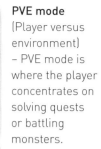

PVE mode (Player versus environment) – PVE mode is where the player concentrates on solving quests or battling monsters.

PVP mode (Player versus player) – PVP in this mode duels and battles are played out against other online users.

Mr T insists that he is 'Night Elf-MOHAWK'. The director responds by reminding him there is no Mohawk class. Mr T is adamant that he can be a Mohawk as well as a Night Elf. It is clear that he has invested personally in his avatar and sees it as a representation of himself. His final comment is to tell the director to 'Shut up fool!' In another commercial, the robed William Shatner discloses he is a Shaman. His final comment is that 'on *Warcraft* you can be anyone you want, dog'. This reminds us that representations of characters in these MMORPGs are clearly linked to representations of who you are and what class you are. It is more personal than taking on the role of a prescribed avatar such as Mario or Lara Croft.

NPC (Non Player Characters) – these are the people of Azeroth who give quests, offer services and exist to provide the 'back story' of the game.

TASK

Create a new avatar for a fantasy game like *World of Warcraft* under the following headings:

- Appearance/dress.
- Personality.
- Special powers and weaknesses.

Consider how colours, costume and accessories can help you to create your avatar. What are the connotations of your choices?

Explore the ways in which your character reinforces or challenges typical representations of gender within games.

Narrative and play

The structure of games is another feature for us to examine as they are split into levels, worlds, laps, rounds and areas of play. In *World of Warcraft* a player will emerge into a certain area depending on the type of character they are. This immediate or 'birthing' world is one a new player may explore with little fear of running into much trouble. As an inexperienced level one Night Elf you may learn about your character, build your hunting skills by attacking the relatively harmless wild boar and eventually work out how to accept quests from the NPC characters.

There is of course the possibility that you may wish to leave this world immediately and aim for Lordaeron or Central Kalimdor. However, this is not to be advised as you are almost certain to be attacked by Orcs or Trolls or the much more complex (higher level) creatures you are not equipped to fight. You are certain to die and have to start all over again. The structure of the game, then, while allowing some narrative freedom, clearly directs and guides the player in these early stages. There are clearly defined rules of play in both PVP and PVE options and are there to be discovered through play.

TASK

How does the narrative progress / flow in computer games? Take a game of your choice and plot the development of your character. Consider the movement between levels, what is required to progress, what challenges or problems you may meet along the way and when and where the narrative ends.

Games are spatial and when analysing them you need to consider how this space is created and used. *World of Warcraft* is set in the fictional world of Azeroth, but this virtual space is also under attack from others, or is forever being contested. The space is changed when moving from PVE to PVP modes and the nature of the contest is prioritised.

Space is a part of all games and narrative spaces are often selling points of games, because the emphasis may fall on how many levels or screens a game may have. The game world is constantly growing and two-dimensional spaces are rapidly being overtaken by three-dimensional spaces which exist in a persistent state. Conventional analytical terms such as 'narrative structure' do not sit as comfortably within this world. However, it is not that we cannot and should not use this, or that we should ignore all the aspects of the games' narrative, but rather that they may not necessarily fit into the more traditional narrative structures and therefore we need to develop and refine our understanding of these areas.

Users and the MMORPG

Media texts are considered to be polysemic and can be read / used in many different ways by different audiences. If we consider how games texts are constructed we could apply Stuart Hall's theory of preferred reading ('Encoding: Decoding', 1980) to the ways users may respond (although there is no doubt that the makers of *Warcraft*, Blizzard, desire their game to be read / played in a certain way and for audience / users to conform to certain rules). In a world where your character has a degree of free will there is always the potential to ignore the encoded meaning or expected mode of behaviour. In *Warcraft* this form of aberrant behaviour is known as 'ganking' or going after inexperienced or lower level players. Whilst this is not entirely illegal, it is not a way to earn respect. 'Griefing' is another aberrant form of play. This is where a player ignores the objectives defined by the game world and instead seeks to harass or cause grief to other players. A recent episode of *South Park* deals with just such negative play. 'Make Love, Not Warcraft' shows the boys being killed in PVP mode by a griefer. Makers Blizzard are forced to become involved in a desperate attempt to save the World [*of Warcraft*] by passing on a secret sword.

South Park: Make Love, Not Warcraft

Ideas about narrative and individual control become especially pertinent here. Can we approach *World of Warcraft* as narrative in the traditional sense or should we be thinking more about the concept of 'play' as purported by ludologists such as Espen, Aarseth, Gonzalo Frasca and Jesper Juul?

TASK

Explore 'griefing' and other rogue forms of play by using internet sites, games chatrooms and blogs. To what extent do they disrupt the expected narrative flow of the game?

Often the typical perception of a gamer is male, usually a lone teenager who spends endless hours alone in his bedroom blasting his way through alien worlds, gunning down innocent bystanders or driving recklessly and with great speed. Gamers are often represented as being anti-social and isolated. It has been suggested that the dangers of excessive gaming could be anything from demonstrating a lack of social skills to actually being influenced to behave in a mindlessly violent way.

However, the nature of gaming itself is changing and the whole idea of the lone gamer hidden away in their (his) room is one that no longer appears credible. Firstly, many more girls are now also playing games. Games like *The Sims* and MMORPG's like *World of Warcraft* are making sure of this. Secondly, more and more people are coming on-line and playing games across the world together. You are now likely to be part of a huge on-line community where you can interact with a variety of other global users. In *World of Warcraft*, PVP mode allows you to test your character against another player in another part of the virtual (and real) world. Players also use forums and chatrooms to communicate about the game, about specific characters and quests or the latest upgrades and patches. Surrounding *World of Warcraft* is a very large virtual community and users can enhance their enjoyment of the game with a range of post-game activities or experiences such as fan art, comic strips and storytelling.

Like many popular games, *World of Warcraft* has expanded into other markets such as film, board games and comics. *The South Park* episode, 'Make Love Not Warcraft', gives an indication of the effect of the game on popular culture. In 2009, a film version of the game with a $100 million budget behind it is scheduled for release. Games are big business and appear to have a thriving life beyond the game itself. Action figures, trading cards, board games, T-shirts and a whole range of other merchandise can also be bought by fans.

TASK

Explore the impact of changing technologies on gaming. Consider how this has affected:

- The production of games like *World of Warcraft*.

- The impact of convergence and how the internet, satellite and mobile communications have affected production, distribution and marketing.

- How audiences / users are positioned.

TASK

1. Select two games. How have they been advertised and marketed? Explore how and where they were publicised (TV adverts, cinema, specialist magazine, internet).

2. How important is the marketing of a game to its success?

Tomb Raider

Lara Croft and the *Tomb Raider* games are amongst the most successful and well-known games franchises to-date. The original *Tomb Raider* was launched in 1996 by British company Eidos as an alternative to the traditional all male-led games that previously dominated the games world. In his book, *Trigger Happy*, Steven

Poole (2000) comments that prior to Lara it was widely believed in the industry that female characters never sold. Lara proved that this was not the case. She sold over 28 million units worldwide and to-date has accrued more than $1 billion in retail sales. She embarked on further adventures with *Tomb Raider Anniversary* and *Tomb Raider Underworld*. The launch of these games has once again seen Lara on the covers of magazines, in the press and keeping up to date with modern technology by launching her own My Space page. Lara has undergone many changes since she first appeared, but her marketability and popularity have not diminished.

Looking at Lara – Representation of women in games

Helen W. Kennedy (2002) poses the question of whether a character like Lara Croft provides girls with an inspirational role model or is she nothing but a cyber bimbo in hotpants? The representation of women in games has long been a controversial issue. For many years female avatars have been shown as either props or bystanders; they are often heavily sexualised like *Ridge Racer*'s Reiko Nagase or Joanna Dark, or offered as rewards and prizes to be won by the more dominant male characters. Lara Croft provides a different representation of women for the world of gaming.

Lara's creator Toby Gard admits that she 'showed some skin' (*The Guardian*, 15th June, 2001) but he maintains that her wardrobe is practical and was a deliberate reaction to the spangly thongs, S&M corsets and spirally metal bras that many female games characters wear. Lara's presence as a female lead in a very male dominated world, even over a decade later, is in itself challenging and her action-packed exploits do indeed question typical, and stereotypical, gender roles.

However, despite being received positively by many women gamers, the shameless sexualised marketing of Lara and some of the close-up and personal camera shots in the game also turned off women gamers. Feminist critic Elaine Showalter sees Lara as being an idealised character that 'no real woman can ever hope to equal' and worries that 'young girls will grow even more dissatisfied with their own bodies' because of her (quoted in: Lara Croft: Feminist Icon or Cyber Bimbo? by Helen W. Kennedy). Female gamers on the forum of www.womengamers.com commented that the camera's focus on Lara's crotch when she swims, or the shower scene in *Tomb Raider 3* when she coyly asks 'Haven't you seen enough?' before disappearing from view, were more for the titillation of a male audience than about representing a female action hero.

It has been suggested that the representation of women within the industry is one of the reasons why women don't play games. Certainly there will be female gamers who don't want to regard women characters just as prizes or victims, and this emphasises the point that different users may respond differently to games and that gender is just one of the reasons why this is the case. But does this actually stop girls gaming? There is evidence to suggest that this is not necessarily the case. Women make up a large part of the games market in the UK – just over a quarter of the total number of gamers. ELSPA figures show that this rises to 39% in the US and 69% in Korea.

ELSPA - the Entertainment & Leisure Software Publishers Association founded in 1989 to establish a specific and collective identity for the British computer and video game industry.

It is not so much that women are not gaming but rather that they appear to be playing by their own rules and in their own ways – less of the 'hack and slash' and more 'pick up and play'. This may partly be dictated by the lack of leisure time available to them and women, it would appear, want less complex controls and more depth to the story and the character. *The Legend of Zelda*, *The Sims* and *The Prince of Persia* all score strongly amongst women, raising interesting questions about the nature of games targeted at women. In trying to develop and expand into the women's market for games, companies have apparently developed games that are feminine in appeal and appear to reinforce ideological gender stereotypes.

Consider the range of Barbie games that deal with fashion shows, pet shows and horse riding competitions; or the virtual pet keeping, *Nintendogs*. These titles reinforce nurturing roles for girls and do not, like many other games, prioritise competition or conflict. But, why are girls (and their mothers) so willing to accept a return to such traditional values? If Lara could be seen as a postmodern example of female representation in 1996 then what does the success of fairy princess Barbie in 2008 imply about how women perceive their place in the games world and beyond?

Lara Croft and industry

Lara has been a marketing dream for many years. She was perhaps the first game character to move from being the object of a substantial advertising and marketing campaign to being a 'virtual' celebrity in her own right, becoming the vehicle for the promotion of an entirely different product. The Lucozade campaign of 2000 saw Lara taking on the promotion of a drink that had hitherto been seen as a tonic for the ill or the elderly. As the (male) gamer takes a break so does Lara. After refreshing her energy levels with Lucozade she is able to fight on with renewed vigour. In another advert of the 'Gone a Bit Lara' campaign 'wannabe' Laras (this time real women dressed as the heroine) navigate the hazards of the more mundane real world thanks to the extra energy provided by their drink of choice.

Accompanying Lara's performance were celebrity appearances on the front covers of fashion and lifestyle magazines. Lara appeared on the cover of *The Face* (June 1997), appeared in digital form on U2's Pop Mart tour and had a book dedicated to her in 1998 when cult author Douglas Copeland produced a series of essays about the fictional star.

TASK

Draw up a list of game characters aside from Lara Croft that have been involved in advertising products.

Consider the ways in which other media forms are linked to the games industry:

- Advertising.
- Magazines.
- Film.

What is the impact of this convergence on gaming?

Games based on films and vice versa have become more and more common. The game versions of successful blockbusters or television programmes are to be found everywhere, often released simultaneously. Often the source material is prioritised to the detriment of the playability of the game. Similarly Hollywood continues to license videogames in the hope of capturing a global audience of gamers. Attracting a pre-existing fan base is a way of ensuring success for your film and as games become more narrative- and character-centred this becomes a more plausible possibility. The original *Tomb Raider* film (2001) starring Angelina Jolie was one of the more commercially successful game spin-offs. This was followed by a second film, *The Cradle of Life* (2003). Between them, these films have grossed more than $450 million at the box office. However, the formula for success of the *Tomb Raider* films is hard to pinpoint. Some believe the draw of Angelina Jolie was the main

Cut Scene – a scene over which the player has no control. Often these scenes contain narrative information and form a cut or break in the narrative for players.

reason, but it has also been suggested that the games themselves have a cinematic quality which translates well to the big screen. What is clear is that the films were able to attract a wider and more diverse audience than the original games and this, in turn, encouraged film-goers to become game players. Other games franchises have been equally successful; despite poor critical reception *Resident Evil* (2002) was a big box office hit. However, a built-in fan base is not always sufficient to guarantee success; the $70 million box office flop *Doom* (2005) was a notable failure.

One thing is clear, however: the link between films and games is here to stay. Games adverts and cut scenes become ever more 'filmic', indeed some games' 'cut' scenes are very complicated and are becoming more elaborate. The games industry continues to provide ready-made narratives and heroes for film-makers. Perhaps one of the defining moments in the development of this game / film marriage is the involvement of producer Jerry Bruckheimer (of the *Pirates of the Caribbean* franchise) in the Disney film, *Prince of Persia* (2009). According to *Edge* magazine, such a big name with a celebrated track record 'gives the genre of videogame movies a kind of legitimacy'. (www.edge-on-line.com/magazine).

TASK

Watch the *Tomb Raider Anniversary* games trailer. Compare it to the film trailer for either of the *Tomb Raider* films. Analyse both texts, considering the following:

- Genre.
- Narrative.
- Representation.
- Technical and audio codes.

How does the games trailer make use of conventions we would associate with film? What features of the game are evident in the film trailer?

How do audiences respond to film versions of games? Use *Tomb Raider* websites, fansites and chatrooms to discover what audiences think.

Bully

Bully, the third-person, school-based game, was released on 4 March 2008 for the Nintendo Wii and X-Box 360. *Bully the Scholarship Edition* is the latest in a line of controversial texts from Rockstar Games, producers of the *Grand Theft Auto* series. *Bully* and the reception it has received have once again divided opinion about the role of violence in games and the effects that this may have on audiences.

In *Bully*, the player takes on the role of Jimmy Hopkins, a 15 year-old tearaway who has been sent to the fictional Bullworth academy to mend his ways. Here cliques abound and we see a variety of social groups represented, including jocks, preppies, nerds and bullies, as well as powerful prefects and, most disturbingly, the unhinged teaching staff. As Jimmy, you must attempt to attend your lessons and receive an education while at the same time avoiding the bullies who are attempting to pummel you, the girls who are vying for your attention and the nerds who need help with their science project.

Teen Tearaways – Representation and Youth

Perhaps one of the reasons that a game like *Bully* attracts so much negative attention is that it deals with the representation of the teenager. Teenagers have always been difficult to pin down in media texts and games are no different.

TASK

Look at current representations of teenagers across a range of media texts (newspapers, film, TV, magazines). How are they depicted? In what way are these representations positive or negative?

Are there any other games that represent teenagers? How does the representation reinforce or challenge current media representations?

Bully is structured like the *Grand Theft Auto* franchise, and like most of these third-person action / adventure games, there are tasks to complete and challenges to unlock. The user is required to escort a nerd through bully-infested halls to earn more popularity points or else play some pranks and try to blame the mischief on someone else. You attend lessons, take photos for the yearbook and even chat up girls. All these things seem to be quite ordinary and uncontroversial, but they have not prevented the game from attracting opprobrium.

In the UK the game is rated '15'. There is no blood, no-one gets seriously hurt or dies. There is a lot of fighting and many of the tasks require you to be adept at violence but there is also a clear sense of morality to the game and there are sanctions and punishments when behaviour is deemed unacceptable. Discipline is enforced by the prefects and other authority figures and attacking smaller children, girls or teachers is not tolerated and leads you to be immediately apprehended. The game, it would seem, offers no more alarming characters or situations than an average episode of *Hollyoaks* or *The OC*. However, it would appear that the fact that this is a game and not a television drama has led to bitter and vitriolic condemnation. Conflict and its resolution are apparently acceptable in films or television programmes; in computer games they are not. While it is accepted that bullying is a real part of many students' lives, tackling these issues in fictional form is only appropriate as long as it not done via the virtual world of the computer game.

Bare-knuckle contest in The OC

However, the user is not encouraged to attack innocent bystanders or undertake acts of bullying and there is no reward to be gained from 'bullying'. In fact many of the tasks are actively about thwarting bullies. This is not to say that the game acts as a moral compass from which we should all take direction, and with the new Wii version there will no doubt be some who disapprove of the motion senser controls being used to deliver the blows.

Bully started its life contentiously when the name itself resulted in assumptions being made about the game and its content. Labour MP Keith Vaz and the UK charity Bullying Online called for the game to be banned. Vaz stated that we should 'consider a game featuring school bullying in the same way we treat a violent film' and urged the government to ban the game whose contents 'sounded disturbing' (http://news.bbc.co.uk/1/hi/uk-politics/4380020.stm). He was backed by Liz Carnell, director of Bullying Online, who commented in *The Guardian*, 'Bullying is not a joke. It is not a suitable subject for computer games' (http://news.bbc.co.uk/1/hi/uk-politics/4380020.stm). In America, campaigning Florida lawyer Jack Thompson succeeded in persuading Wal Mart to stop pre-selling the game which was at the time un-certificated. He called the game a 'Columbine simulator' (quoted in *Washington Post* article by Mike Musgrove 12th October, 2006).

All of this was pre-release. Even Presidential candidate Hillary Clinton attacked Rockstar saying these games 'steal the innocence of our children and [make] the job of being a parent harder' (http://www.senate.gov/~clinton/news/statements/details.cfm?id=240603). Not one of these individuals had actually played the game.

Rockstar responded by urging people not to judge the game by its name or individual scenes taken out of context. The game was referred to the British Board of Film Classification (BBFC) and received a '15' rating. Perhaps bowing to public pressure, Rockstar renamed the European version of the Play Station 2 game *Canus Canem Edit*, using the 'dog eat dog' motto of Bullworth. Despite this, continued protests and disputes concerning the nature of the game and then the wider debate about the effect of violent video games in general ensued.

Rockstar, publishers of *Bully* and the much debated *Grand Theft Auto* (*GTA*) series, are no strangers to controversy. The *Grand Theft Auto* games have always raised questions about what is appropriate content and subject matter for games. The adult nature of the game and some of the gang-related or sexual violence contained within some of the editions have had many calling for games such as *GTA* to be banned completely. Others would be content with stricter and more stringent controls for the classification and selling of such games (for a thorough discussion of *GTA*, see McDougall and O'Brien, 2008).

Similarly, in 2004 the Rockstar game *Manhunt* was withdrawn from retailers following the brutal murder of Stefan Pakeerah at the hands of 17 year-old Warren LeBlanc. Pakeerah had been stabbed and beaten with a claw hammer. The media made the decision quickly that the game was to blame. *The Daily Mail* ran the headline 'Murder by Playstation' (29th July, 2004) and the *Guardian* too suggested that the murder had been 'incited' by *Manhunt*. ELSPA (the Entertainment and Leisure Software Association) issued a statement in response to the news coverage. In it they stated: 'We reject the suggestion or association between the tragic events in the Midlands and the sale of the videogame *Manhunt*.' (5th August, 2004).

This did not stop the media coverage which became more and more inflammatory. However, the evidence linking *Manhunt* to the murder was much less clear-cut than was implied by these reports, with the police ultimately ruling out any connection at all.

What is clear is the fact that there is a definite anxiety about the content of computer games and the effect they may have on gamers. The debate about whether violent games make us more violent appears to have replaced the concern about 'video nasties' in the 1980s. Ideas about the media and its harmful effects are nothing new.

The Columbine High School massacre – the massacre took place in 1999, at Columbine High School in Colorado. Two students, Eric Harris and Dylan Klebold, shot and killed 12 students and a teacher, as well as wounding 23 others, before committing suicide.

Rockstar Games (also known as Rockstar NYC) – a development division of video game publisher Take-Two Interactive, based in Edinburgh, Scotland.

Are we a more violent society as a result of playing endless 'beat 'em ups' and war games? The answer, it would appear, is... we don't know. It may even be a reductive question to ask what the effects of violence are when there are so many different types of violence in different contexts.

Some research makes links between violent games and 'real world' aggression, yet other research can find no strong effects or any evidence to support a link. What is more certain, perhaps, is the need to look into this more closely. Steven Johnson comments that 'the one thing that we know for certain is this: if there is some positive correlation between exposure to fictional violence and violent behaviour, its effects are by definition much weaker than other social trends that shape violence in society' (Everything bad for you is good for you, Steven Johnson, Riverhead, 2005). Dmitri Williams from the University of Illinois talks of the need for 'policy makers [to] seek a greater understanding of the games they are debating. It may be that the attackers and defenders of the industry's products are operating without enough information, and are instead both arguing for blanket approaches to what is likely to be a more complicated phenomenon'. (http://www.theregister.co.uk/2005/08/15/video_games_and_aggression/) British prime minister Gordon Brown has made steps towards this greater understanding by commissioning Dr Tanya Byron to enquire into the role of videogames in children's lives and their effects. The Byron Report was published in spring 2008 and broadly welcomed by all sides of the debate.

Even gamers themselves are not clear on this subject. Looking at chatrooms and fan sites, some appear to agree that more regulation is needed as some games may be inappropriate for some players; whereas some gamers feel that they are easily able to distinguish between virtual and real world violence.

At the time of writing *Bully* has just been re-released by Rockstar. It is no longer called *Canus Canem* but has reverted to its original controversial title. As yet there have been no further calls to ban it: perhaps its opponents, having actually seen the content of the game, have decided that there is no need to call for its ban or perhaps we are becoming more accepting of the games world and the themes explored by the games. Yet one senses that, in the absence of hard evidence one way or the other, the debate about audiences and violence and games is here to stay.

TASK

- Research some of the articles about *Bully*. Do you think there is sufficient evidence to support banning this game? To what extent is the response a media-generated panic?

- Have a class debate about violence and videogames and whether they should be banned.

- How are videogames currently classified or rated? How useful is the current ratings and classification system?

TASK

With reference to the three games you have studied, explore the ways in which they use gender representations. You might like to consider some of the following points:

- Women as role models.

- Women as victims.

- Men as heroes.

- Men as villains.

Bibliography

Atkins, B. (2003) *More Than a Game: The Computer Game as Fictional Form*, Manchester University Press: Manchester

Carr, D. & Buckingham, D & Burn, A & Schott, G., (2006) *Computer Games Text: Narrative and Play*, Polity Press: Cambridge

Howson, G., (2006) *Lara's Creator Speaks*. guardian.co.uk/technology [internet]. April 18th. Available at: HYPERLINK "http://blogs.guardian.co.uk/games/archives/2006/04/18/laras_creator_speaks.html" http://blogs.guardian.co.uk/games/archives/2006/04/18/laras_creator_speaks.html [accessed January 20th 2008]

Johnson, S., (2005) *Everything Bad Is Good For You*, Penguin: London

Kennedy, H., (2002) *Lara Croft Feminist Icon Or Cyber Bimbo: On The Limits Of Textual Analysis*. International Journal of Computer Game Research. Vol 2. Issue 2. [internet] Available at http://www.gamestudies.org/0202/kennedy/

Kitts, M., (2008) *Review Bully- Scholarship Edition*. N-Gamer Magazine, Issue 21 p.48-53

McDougall, J. and O'Brien, W. (2008) *Studying Videogames*, Auteur Publishing: Leighton Buzzard

Meadows, M S., (2008) *I, Avatar: The Consequences Of Having A Second Life*, Pearson Education: Oxford

Mott, T. ed., *Reel Gaming*. Edge Magazine. Issue 186. p. 74-81

Newman, J & Oram, B., (2006) *Teaching Videogames*, BFI Publishing: London

Poole, S., (2000) *Trigger Happy: Videogames And The Entertainment Revolution*, Arcade Publishing Inc: New York

Websites

www.elspa.com

www.theesa.com

www.blizzard.com

www.tombraider.com/anniversary

www.bit-tech.net

www.womengamers.com

www.imdb.com

www.dcsf.gov.uk/byronreview

www.theregister.co.uk

Film

Vivienne Clark

This section will focus on three films – *The Bourne Ultimatum* (Paul Greengrass, US/Germany, 2007), *Atonement* (Joe Wright, UK/France, 2007) and *This is England* (Shane Meadows, UK, 2006) – as a way of exploring films, their audiences and the industries which produce, distribute and exhibit them.

When you study any film, you will be concentrating on genre, narrative and representation, the major textual features of any media product. But you will also be asking questions about what those films reveal about audiences (how they are targeted and how different audiences respond to films, for example) and about the industry which produces and distributes them. This section looks at textual issues selectively – concentrating mainly on genre issues through *The Bourne Ultimatum*, narrative perspectives through *Atonement* and representation through *This is England*. Some of the key industry and audience issues which these films raise will be also be considered. The section should provide you with a good starting point for exploring film and beginning to ask questions about the relationship between 'texts', their audiences and the industry which underlies them.

Genre – balance between industry and audience needs?

There are two important areas to explore when studying genre:

- How does the film industry use genre?

- What does genre offer audiences?

The film industry generally uses genre fairly simply – as a means of minimising the risk of failure. Genre allows the film industry to produce the kinds of film it thinks audiences will like, predicting future success based on what has already been commercially successful. Genre follows the principle of repeating and varying conventions – the elements which audiences like and therefore want to see again. This tendency to repeat based on previous commercial success often results in the emergence of a trend for a particular genre. For example, the considerable popular and critical success of Ridley Scott's classical epic, *Gladiator* (Ridley Scott, UK/USA, 2000), spawned a succession of similar 'sword and sandal' movies, such as Troy (Wolfgang Petersen, USA/Malta/UK, 2004) and *Alexander* (Oliver Stone, Germany/USA/Netherlands, UK, 2004).

Film franchises work in a similar way. If a character is popular with audiences, the film industry will often produce sequels, TV spin-offs and merchandise, extending the brand and maximising the money they will generate from fans. The Bourne films reflects this trend as the franchise already includes a videogame, *The Bourne Conspiracy* (2008), and a further, fourth film is now planned to capitalise on the success of the original trilogy. As Greengrass himself said of the unresolved ending

Production
– The technical production of the film as well as the finance required to produce it.

Distribution
– release strategies, production of prints and DVDs, marketing and promotion of films.

Exhibition
– the screening of films...at cinemas, on television or 'home cinemas' and (increasingly) on the internet.)

of *The Bourne Ultimatum*: 'I want [Bourne] to survive; you never know when you might need him' (DVD commentary).

Genre can also be used creatively by screenwriters and directors who can extend and vary genre conventions as well as subvert or even parody them, as Wes Craven's *Scream* series (USA, 1996, 1997, 2000) did with the horror genre. But even this technique, new and fun when it first emerged, can become formulaic as the *Scary Movie 1* and *2* (Keenen Ivory Wyans, USA, 2000 and 2001) and *I Know What You Did Last Summer* (Jim Gillespie, USA, 1997) and spin-off series of films have shown.

The way the film industry uses genres could suggest that audiences are exploited and turned into passive consumers. However it can be equally argued that audiences actively choose the films they watch and that whilst many genres offer audiences something that is familiar, they gain pleasure from having their expectations fulfilled. What audiences seem to like most, however, is the familiar with slight variations. If a genre become too formulaic, audiences tend to lose interest; they constantly want to be reassured by the expected and yet challenged by the unexpected.

> **'Whereas each individual car made according to the specifications of any one model should, ideally, be identical to all the others, each individual film belonging to a particular genre has to be different'.** Neale, 1980, p 52

You could say, therefore, that genre is a balance between the industry's financial need for profit and audiences' needs for entertainment and pleasure.

Audience responses to genre can often appear contradictory. They like the familiar and the reassurance that genre conventions provide and yet they also become easily bored and are constantly demanding a degree of variety and innovation. Therefore, Hollywood has to extend, develop or even break genre conventions rather than rigidly adhering to an established formula.

> **' genres are paradoxically placed as simultaneously conservative and innovative in so far as they respond to the expectations that are industry – and audience –based.'** Hayward, 2006, p160

Hollywood often raids other national cinemas in order to find that significant and fresh approach to a genre. You might think of the way the horror genre was refreshed by re-making Japanese films with *The Ring* (Gore Verbinski, UK/Japan, 2002) and *Dark Water* (Walter Salles, US, 2005). Film-makers also increasingly merge genres, creating hybrids. This mixing of conventions from different genres can help create films that are familiar but less formulaic. For example *Brick* (2005) set its Film Noir narrative in the world of Teen movies creating something new for fans of both genres. This process of subverting and mixing conventions has led to a new view of genre as a whole. Rather than seeing genre as simple fixed categories that texts can be divided up into, genre is now seen as a fluid, evolving set of relationships. David Buckingham argues that **'genre is not... simply "given" by the culture: rather, it is in a constant process of negotiation and change'** (http://www.aber.ac.uk/media/Documents/intgenre/intgenre1.html).

The use of genre conventions in the marketing of films similarly reflects the need for both repetition and difference. Posters frequently use a film's genre to attract audiences - the images which are used, the choice of stars, the producer, director, taglines, typefaces and even colours can help indicate the genre of a film to a potential audience. However, marketing campaigns also aim to ensure that each film stands out from the competition. Unique selling points, such as stars, can be used to make films seem different and appealing but many posters will also showcase how the film deviates from the established formula of a genre, aiming to both maintain the interest of established fans and to develop a following from new fans.

TASK

Collect three contrasting, recent Hollywood film posters.

- What genre codes and conventions can you identify in them?

- Do any of the posters suggest that the film draws on more than one genre?

- How far is genre used to market the films?

- What other elements are included to help market the films?

The Bourne Ultimatum and the Bourne trilogy: Genre - repetition, variation and hybridity

The Bourne trilogy of films provides an interesting example of this balance between industry and audience needs. Even though some of the standard conventions of the action genre are still present for audiences to enjoy, the Bourne films demonstrate several departures from mainstream Hollywood action movie conventions. For example, the films appear far more aware of international politics than many traditional action films, and, they appear to integrate action into the narrative in a plausible way without the overuse of CGI which has become a reconised signifier of so many action films.

Clearly the Bourne trilogy represents a hybrid version of the action genre, an increasingly common approach in many contemporary Hollywood genre films. Marketed as a 'Bond for a new generation', the Bourne trilogy combines elements from the action/spectacle/adventure and thriller genres, with elements from the political/conspiracy and espionage thriller. These various elements are densely packed into the Bourne films to produce a multi-layered style of film-making, which is somewhat different from a conventional Hollywood action film like *Die Hard 4* (Len Wiseman, UK/USA, 2007).

You can see hybridity as well as a repetition and variation of conventions in the suspense sequence set at Waterloo Station in *The Bourne Ultimatum* (DVD: 16:01 to 26:41). The sequence, which crosscuts from Waterloo Station to CIA surveillance headquarters in New York, features a number of standard conventions of the action and thriller genres including the use of characters, narrative, *mise-en-scène*,

The Bourne trilogy of films consists of: *The Bourne Identity*, Doug Liman, 2002, USA / Germany / Czech Republic, *The Bourne Supremacy*, Paul Greengrass, 2004, US Germany and *The Bourne Ultimatum*, Paul Greengrass, 2007, USA / Germany.

The Internet Movie database defines the genre of *The Bourne Ultimatum* as an Action, Adventure, Mystery, Thriller. Wikipedia refers to it as ' a spy film' (http://en.wikipedia.org/wiki/The_Bourne_Ultimatum_(film))

camerawork/editing and sound.

A set of conventions / expectations, such as the one below, can provide a useful framework for analysis and help you gain a fuller understanding of a scene, in this case the way *The Bourne Ultimatum* uses genre conventions.

- *Characters* - a hero, a villain, the villain's accomplice and a victim.

- *Narrative* - a plot involving political intrigue, a mystery to uncover, an international dimension, usually based in the recognisable present.

- *Mise-en-scène* - a location which offers ample possibilities for putting the hero at risk.

- *Camerawork* - varied camerawork featuring spectacular action, usually involving weapons and death-defying stunts.

- *Editing* - rapid intercutting between key locations and people, to increase audience tension and suspense.

- *Sound design* - a suspenseful orchestral musical score.

The sequence contrasts the mise-en-scène of the CIA offices in New York, essentially the 'hub' of all surveillance operations, with the rendezvous of Bourne and reporter Ross (amidst numerous commuters in Waterloo station). The scenes inside the CIA offices are filmed with a handheld camera, which is unusual for a Hollywood action movie, although the use of close-ups on Vosen representing pressure is more conventional. These offices are appropriately shadowy (for dark deeds), dominated by traditionally masculine colours of black, brown, blue and grey, with no natural light; their faces are lit by the overhead strip lighting, desk lights and the reflections of the many computer screens, monitors and projector screens that crowd the office.

The theme of surveillance, more conventional of the conspiracy or espionage thriller, is evident in the cinematography. The sequence in Waterloo station uses shots from every conceivable angle, including aerial and low angle, wide and close as well as master shots to retain an overview so that the audience can see the geography of the sequence. The camera is dynamic, almost a narrative element within the sequence itself, with fast zooms in and out, tracks and pans to follow Bourne and Ross. It peeps from behind bars and glass, giving us fleeting glimpses of the action, as Bourne systematically eliminates the mobile teams following Ross, so increasing tension.

The editing is conventional for an action movie in that it creates intense excitement through the pacy rhythm of successive shots. Too much pace can impede narrative clarity, so the editing tempo is varied to ensure that the audience is generally clear about who is who and what is happening. However, the tempo of transitions in this and many scenes in *The Bourne Ultimatum* is higher than in most films, meaning the audience experiences the dizzying rush of the chase, whilst just about following the course of events. This is especially important when a new threat, the assassin Paz, is introduced into the mix. It is almost as if Bourne is the director here, calling the 'shots', as he directs Ross's every movement around the station, while the team in the CIA offices can only watch passively on their screens, like the audience itself.

As such the film uses a recognisable set of conventions but does so in a way to breathe life into a scene we have seen many times before.

The sound design faithfully recreates the echo and background noise of the cavernous train station and amplifies the click and clunk of every closing car door and a cold metallic graze of steel on steel in the assembly and loading of weapons, and when combat is involved, we hear every crunch of bone with clinical clarity. When Paz's bullet finds its target in Ross's skull, all sound stops very briefly to mark the moment. Then the final part of this chase sequence commences, with Bourne pursuing Paz through the station into the underground to the serpentine rhythms of Arabic-style music, anticipating the later chase sequence in Tunisia. High-quality sound design has become a feature of Hollywood blockbusters, reflecting audience expectations and technological progress.

TASK

- Look closely at this suspense sequence [16:01 – 26:41].

- Compare the sequence with what you think of as a conventional action thriller (for example, *Die Hard 4* or a Bond film). What is different about *The Bourne Ultimatum* sequence from conventional action thrillers (what are the 'variations on the conventional')? Give your reasons.

- How do these differences relate to the concept of hybrids?

Abu Ghraib:
US prison in Iraq where US army personnel were accused of torturing Iraqi prisoners of war. Graphic images of this torture were released in newspapers in 2004.

Genre and issues of representation in *The Bourne Ultimatum*

A central aspect of the narrative of *The Bourne Ultimatum* is a challenging representation of the US Government and its practices. This is largely presented as a binary opposition between the negatively represented US authorities and the positively represented Jason Bourne, an individual searching for the identity which was stripped from him under questionable circumstances.

The basic opposition of an individual versus an organisation is conventional of the action movie. It helps the audience identify with the underdog who uses their individual traits of courage and resourcefulness to triumph despite the odds. In films such as the *Die Hard* franchise the individual hero represents good - meaning they embody American values and thus offer audiences reassurance in the form of a happy ending in which they defeat some foreign threat. However, contemporary thrillers have become increasingly critical of the US government reflecting the audience's lack of faith in the morality of our leaders and institutions. Jason Bourne is an action hero but one caught up in conflict with the shadowy institutions of his own country rather than with terrorists from another. A close look at the binary oppositions contained in film texts allows us to examine the ideology of films and in this case observe how films go some way to reflecting the attitudes of audiences at a specific time in history.

The use of camerawork and mise-en-scène in all three films underline this negative representation of the US authorities, who act as if they are above the law and beyond accountability. Tracking shots represent sinister, silver-haired CIA staff barking orders at stressed junior operatives. And the flashback sequences, which portray Bourne's returning memories of his initial programming process, similarly represent government agencies harshly. These sequences, which feature Bourne in handcuffs, head covered by a black hood and repeatedly plunged into a water tank to the point of drowning, reference the many images of hooded and humiliated prisoners at Abu Ghraib. Not only do these representations challenge and criticise government methods, they gain added force by drawing on images of well-known, illegal interrogation methods portraying the US Government as a repressive force. The blurred and grainy CCTV shots which follow Bourne across Europe to the US (in streets, banks and petrol stations, on trains and in the subway) reinforce the portrayal of governments as repressive forces – reflecting the increasing level of surveillance within Western societies and thus making an ideological point and reflecting the fact that,

'Generic codes and conventions give a preferred reading' (Hayward, 1996, p164).

Of course different audiences may interpret the film in a variety of ways. The preferred reading outlined above may not appeal to all audiences. Clearly the film can also be enjoyed in more simple terms. The spectacle of an individual hero overcoming a series of elaborate and life-threatening obstacles to complete his quest offers pleasure for audiences who might not necessarily buy into the film's underlying ideology.

Atonement: Narrative

Mainstream narratives usually aim to help audiences suspend disbelief. Suspending disbelief means that we deliberately forget that a media text is a fictional representation and treat it as real, at least for the time we are watching it, thus enabling audiences to cry at the end of *Titanic* (1997) and be shocked by the violence in *Hostel* (2005). Since the early days of film, Hollywood studios have aimed to provide this escapism for audiences by using simple, linear narrative structures where the audience is positioned with a hero who is attempting to complete one, clearly-defined, quest.

As a result many approaches to studying film focus on identifying this narrative formula in individual films by dividing them into stages (equilibrium, disruption, etc.) or recognising character functions (hero, villain, princess, etc.). This process can be a useful starting point for understanding how stories are told. However some films have different, more complex narratives for which this type of analysis may be less effective. *Atonement* is a film in which the audience is not simply supposed to suspend disbelief, rather the narrative demands that the audience thinks about how we interpret and gain fulfilment from this and other stories.

The narrative structure depends on recognising that all stories – whether films, novels or plays like the young Briony's *The Trials of Arabella* with which the film opens – are subjective and reflect individuals' perceptions. The narrative of *Atonement* is constructed so that it is clear that there are different, conflicting versions of reality. This means the audience does not completely suspend its disbelief but is encouraged to question the reality of the story. This is done by undermining the audience's trust in the narrator, Briony.

Atonement's narrative follows Briony throughout her life towards her attempt at a final atonement for the lives she destroyed with her 'stories' and her biggest lie ('I saw him'), which deprived her sister and her friend of a 'happy ever after' ending to their life story. The narrative effectively juxtaposes several points of view – including significant strands focused on the young Briony, Robbie, the adult Briony and the dying older Briony. Although the film doesn't draw attention to it, the narrative unfolds in three main sections representing each of those points of view with a final short section reflecting the dying Briony's point of view, one which questions all that has preceded it. This manipulation of narrative has been a feature of several contemporary films and arguably informs much contemporary culture. Such films as *Short Cuts* (Robert Altman, US, 1993), *Pulp Fiction* (Quentin Tarantino, US, 1994), *Crash* (Paul Haggis, US/Germany, 2004) and *Babel* (Alejandro Gonzáles Iñárritu, France/US/Mexico, 2006) all serve to remind us that there is no single authoritative version of any event, of any story.

Atonement is partially about the guilt which arises from a lie and its consequences but the film also explores the logic of recognising that all perceptions of reality are just that – perceptions. This is first made clear to the audience by showing the same scene from two different points of view. (DVD: 6:12 – 12:36). Briony's version of what happens when Cecilia and Robbie meet at the fountain and the vase is broken is shown to be misleading once the audience is positioned with the two characters involved in the exchange and are thus able to hear their conversation and read their body language. The change in perspective alters audiences' perceptions – although, as the film progresses, audiences' perceptions are similarly called into question as well.

At the start of the two versions of this fountain sequence, the sound of a bee, which audiences see in close up as it lands on a window pane, attracts Briony's attention. The shallow depth of focus on the bee is pulled to allow the full depth of field, which reveals Cecilia and Robbie outside standing at the fountain in the garden below. Briony, and the audience, cannot hear what is going on and are reliant on actions and body language seen only in an extreme long shot. From her limited perspective, she misunderstands the situation. She gasps first at Cecilia undressing in front of Robbie and turns away shocked. When she looks again, she gasps once more on seeing Cecilia's near nudity as she emerges wet from the fountain's pool. Briony senses that what she has witnessed is sexual in some way, but jumps to the conclusion, prompted by her own jealousy and other misunderstandings, that Robbie somehow made her do it.

The sequence is then replayed from Cecilia's perspective. Cecilia takes the vase and flowers outside and speaks with Robbie. The relationship between them is hinted at through their brief and tense exchanges, emotions revealed through pauses and glances, by the unspoken. Using medium close-ups and detail shots allows the audience to better understand the nature of their relationship, understanding denied to Briony. As Cecilia emerges from the fountain the frisson of attraction between the two characters is palpable and essential in motivating their strand of the narrative. It is also Briony's inability to comprehend her sister's relationship which motivates her to lie and thus begin the sequence of events within the narrative.

The film then continues with a distinct narrative strand, almost like a new chapter, in which four years have passed and Robbie is fighting in the Second World War. This strand is perhaps the most conventional in that we have a hero, Robbie, with a quest to return home to Cecelia who he loves. The ending of this strand is enigmatic, our hero is stranded at the beach in Dunkirk and the audience is uncertain as to whether he will die or be rescued. It is only when we reach the final section of the film, an interview with Briony, now an elderly novelist, that we discover that Robbie did indeed die at Dunkirk.

The audience is informed by Briony that the previous scenes in which she visited Robbie and Cecilia living together in South London to apologise and attempt to atone for the lie she told are actually fictional. This means that the audience has been watching a chapter from her novel rather than an honest account of events. The scene could not have happened because Robbie never returned, Cecilia was also killed and obviously this means that there was no atonement for Briony. The elderly Briony explains that she changed the story because "…what sense of hope, or satisfaction could a reader derive from an ending like that…"

Atonement has a highly complex narrative structure: it is non-linear; events are represented from different characters' points of view and a distinction is made between the true story and Briony's version of it, but this is only made clear to audiences after they have watched this strand. All these factors encourage the audience to actively question the film rather than simply suspending disbelief. *Atonement* also forces the audience to think about the purpose and pleasure of fiction compared with real life experience. The film audience is given a traditional happy ending but this lacks the same satisfaction as it has learnt previously that this is fantasy.

TASK

After you have watched *Atonement* discuss the following questions:

- Who in the narrative might be considered heroic?

- Do any of the characters have quests, and if so, are they completed?

- How does the ending affect the audience's emotional response to the film?

- Finally, consider how important are happy endings to the success of films.

This is England: Representation

Films – like any media – don't simply provide a window on reality, they offer representations of it – versions of reality. At their simplest, representations are images plus points of view about them. Representations therefore incorporate points of view about the 'reality' they represent. They are therefore ideological and have the power to reinforce the way the majority of people think by constantly reflecting and reinforcing the dominant ideologies. However it is also true that representations can challenge dominant ideologies by presenting alternative points of view.

Representation of time and place

Opening and title sequences are useful for the study of representation as they not only establish central characters, but place them in a social context. This is particularly significant when that social, cultural and historical setting is important to the themes and narrative of the film.

The opening title sequence of *This is England* is a montage of archive footage from 1980s TV – hence its deliberately grainy quality. It is edited to *Toots and the Maytals'* ska track '54-46 (What's my Number?)'. The track was originally released in 1968, then remixed and reissued in 1979 and suggests the early days of skinhead culture (pre-National Front and British National Party associations) to which the film later refers. The font of the titles are produced in a stencil-like typeface, recalling army signs and dog tags. In his DVD commentary, the director Shane Meadows says that the numbers which scroll up under the cast and crew's names are real numbers from the dog tags of deceased British soldiers in the Falklands war, a creative decision which hints at the challenging ideological stance of the film.

The opening montage sequence superficially looks like a 'history' of the major events and popular cultural trends of the early 1980s. It moves from the trivial and absurd (including Roland Rat, an icon of Saturday morning kids' TV, *Space Invaders*, Rubik's cube and *Duran Duran*'s New Romantic hairstyles and make-up) to the increasingly serious (national and political events such as the wedding of Prince Charles and 'Lady Di', anti-US air base protests, the miners' strike, a National Front march down Whitehall and race riots). Throughout the sequence, the Prime Minister of the time, Margaret Thatcher, appears in various contexts as an all-pervading influence. The sequence ends with footage from the Falklands war, with a shocking image of a British soldier being rushed to safety on a stretcher, holding up the bloodied stump of one leg. The final image from the Falklands conflict reminds audiences of that war and links them to the back story of the main character Shaun, whose father was killed there.

The images of course are not a simple 'history': they are a highly selective representation of that era and serve to point to the challenging ideologies the film conveys. Indeed, the representation of the 1980s contained in the film suggests that the impact of the social and political changes made by Margaret Thatcher and her government pervaded all aspects of life, both personal and social, national and international. The construction of this title sequence therefore provides a good example of how a director, through his or her choices, constructs a point of view about 'reality', in this case Britain in the 1980s.

Character representation

The sequence that follows the opening titles introduces audiences to the central character of *This is England*, Shaun, a 12-year old who is growing up on a Nottingham council estate in the 1980s and who is befriended by a tribe of skinheads. The scene begins with Shaun waking up in bed. His room, clothes and later the surrounding streets clearly represent the poverty that Shaun's family live in. Shaun's life is also characterised by conflict: he argues with a shop-owner; is bullied by other boys and ends up in a fight. In the playground the pupils are grouped in clearly defined tribes each with recognisable identities evident in their clothes and haircuts. Shaun stands out from everyone else on the non-uniform day held on the last day at school, as his flared jeans, tan boots and stripy jacket collar are conspicuously out of fashion. He is alone and does not belong to any of the groups of pupils. Most significantly the joke which provokes the fight makes the audience aware that Shaun's father is dead, increasing his sense of isolation.

As we see Shaun struggle to assert himself against this onslaught, the audience can understand the motivation for his desire to be accepted and become part of a group, in this case, by joining the 'family' of skinheads whose leader, Woody, is the only

Margaret Thatcher, conservative Prime Minister from 1979 to 1990. She took Britain to war against Argentina over sovereignty of the Falkland Islands in 1982 and presided over the collapse of the mining industry at a time of mass unemployment. She also introduced a kind of popular capitalism, which provided economic benefits for some.

person to show him positive interest and concern. Shane Meadows constructs the character of Shaun sympathetically. His miserable facial expressions, tatty clothes and small size (especially relative to those he confronts) encourage the audience to feel sorry for him, so they hope that he will find the acceptance and friendship he desperately needs. This sympathy for Shaun is essential for the audience to follow the character as he falls under the influence of the Nazi skin-head Combo.

TASK

- How does Shaun develop as a character throughout the film?

- How is social class represented? What role do social issues such as poverty and unemployment play in the film?

- How is Combo represented in the film? Choose three key moments from the film to support your ideas.

Representation and Audiences: Differential readings

This is England provides a good example of the different ways different audiences can respond to films. Texts generally construct preferred meanings but these are not the only interpretations available to audiences. Various factors influence how audiences decode texts, not least the demographic and psychometric profiles of the audience. For example consider how your ethnic background might influence the way you respond to Combo or your social background might determine the way you interpret the class issues in the film. An audience member's political beliefs will certainly impact on their interpretation of the film given the representation of social issues and Thatcher's influence on 1980's society.

TASK

- Suggest three different audiences for *This is England*.

- How do you think those different audiences will respond to (a) Shaun and (b) Combo?

Representation and regulation

Representation is central to the regulation of film. No theme or issue automatically receives an 18 certificate, rather the BBFC considers the treatment of the subject in terms of its context and the sensitivity of its presentation (http://www.bbfc.co.uk/policy/policy-mainissues.php). However *This is England* received an 18 certificate from the BBFC due to the inclusion of racist violence and language (http://www.bbfc.org.uk/website/Classified.nsf/0/7F3E47CC247AB9A58025727D0037D33F?OpenDocument) even though the film aims to examine this behaviour and its causes. The decision was extremely controversial with the director Meadows arguing that compared with the violence depicted in other films *This is England* should receive a 15 certificate, especially given the important themes the film tackles (http://blogs.guardian.co.uk/film/2007/04/an_18_for_this_is_england_this.html). Bristol council agreed with Meadows and rejected the BBFC's certificate thereby allowing younger audiences to see the film (http://news.bbc.co.uk/1/hi/england/bristol/6601559.stm).

TASK

1. Why do you think the film was awarded this 18 certificate?

2. Do you think the BBFC's decision was justifiable?

3. Is 15 too young to understand the themes represented within the film?

EXTENSION TASK

Consider all three films discussed in this section in terms of their genre and narrative and the ways in which they convey different elements of representation.

- How important is genre in attracting audiences to each of the films?
- Compare and contrast the narrative structures of the three films.
- In what ways do the films offer audiences different pleasures?
- How do each of the films represent the time and place in which they are set?
- How significant are these locations to the narratives of the films?
- Compare and contrast the representation of masculinity in each of the films.
- What different roles do women have in the films?
- To what extent do the 3 films provide audiences with familiarity?

End Notes

Industry issues: Production, distribution and exhibition

All these three films suggest important issues about the industry which you can uncover further through research. This section gives you some starting points.

Look at the table below and note what it suggests about the production, distribution and exhibition of each film.

	The Bourne Ultimatum	*Atonement*	*This is England*
Country or origin – according to production funding	USA / Germany	UK / France	UK
Certificate	12A	15	18
Production companies	Universal Pictures Motion Picture BETA Produktionsgesellschaft The Kennedy / Marshall Company Ludlum Entertainment Bourne Again (uncredited)	Working Title Films Relativity Media Studio Canal	Big Arty Productions EM Media Film4 Optimum Releasing Screen Yorkshire UK Film Council Warp Films
Distribution company (UK & USA)	Universal Pictures	United International Pictures (UIP) Focus Features (US)	Optimum Releasing (theatrical)
Budget – millions (estimated)	$110m (c £75 m)	£30m	£1.5m
Opening weekend USA and UK only / (Number of screens)	$69,283,690 – USA (5/8/07 – 3660 screens) Saturation release £6,553,704 – UK (19/8/07 – 458 screens) Saturation release	$796,836 – USA (9/12/07 – 32 Screens) Narrow release £1,634,065 - UK (9/9/07 – 411 screens) Saturation release	$18,430 – USA (29/7/07 – 1 Screen) Narrow release £207,676 - UK (29/4/07 – 62 screens) Narrow release
Website	www.thebourneultimatum.com	www.atonementthemovie.co.uk	www.thisisenglandmovie.co.uk
Awards won	Oscars ™ 2008: • Best Sound Mixing • Best Sound Editing • Best Film Editing BAFTAS 2008: • Best Editing • Best Sound • 6 nominations	Oscars 2008: • Best Original Score • 7 nominations BAFTAS 2008: • Best Film • Best Production Design • 14 nominations	Oscars 2008: • No nominations BAFTAS: • Best British Film • 2 nominations

TASKS ON PRODUCTION

- What can you find out about *Universal Pictures* and who owns it?

- What do you understand by a 'media conglomerate' and 'vertical and horizontal integration'? How do those relate to the Hollywood film industry today?

- Find out what film and media interests the following have: Vivendi Universal, Time Warner, Sony, Viacom, Disney, News Corporation.

- The distributor ident of *Universal Pictures* opens both *The Bourne Ultimatum* and *Atonement*? Why is this? What are the links between the production and distribution of these films?

TASKS ON DISTRIBUTION

- How do all three films use their official website to attract audiences?

- Explore the trailers for each film (see the Film Distributors' Association website, www.launchingfilms.com for trailers).

- Explore the posters for each film using the posters and prompts on pg. 114.

- What is meant by DVD 'sell-through' and merchandising?

- How are awards used by the film industry and by audiences?

- What do you know about the release patterns of films (for example, narrow, platform, wide and saturation release)?

The Film Distributors' Association is a British organisation representing various companies involved with film distribution; its website (www.launchingfilms.com) has useful data which you can use to study films, including box office statistics, film trailers to download and a micro site (www.launchingfilms.tv) which has videos of industry personnel discussing their roles in film distribution.

TASK

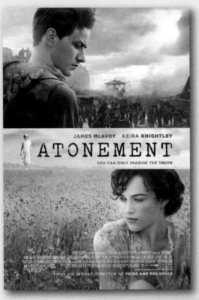

Explore how these posters use genre, stars or other images to attract audiences. Consider the role of the following:

- Images.
- Design and layout.
- Type design.
- Use of colour.
- Language and mode of address.

See if you can find different versions of posters for the films – there are different versions for *The Bourne Ultimatum* and *Atonement*. Explain why you think the different posters were created.

TASKS ON EXHIBITION

- Films are still screened at the cinema (a so-called 'theatrical release'). It is sometimes claimed that the theatrical release of a film is like an advert for DVD sales, games and other merchandising. Can you find examples? How far do you agree?

- Some cinemas are using digital projectors rather than showing (costly) prints of films. What are the advantages and disadvantages of digital exhibition? Do you think cinemas could become giant television screens which use satellites to broadcast recent films? See what you can find out about these ideas.

- In what ways are other forms of exhibition – home cinema, internet downloads – changing viewing habits?

Bibliography

Hayward, S. (2006), *Cinema Studies*, Routledge: Lodon

Neale, S. (1980), *Genre*, BFI Publishing: London

Magazines

Naomi Hodkinson

This section explores three magazine titles which together investigate the areas of genre, narrative and representation. It will also look at the relationships between them, and builds on those understandings in a text-led way. The titles to be explored are *Total Film*, *Grazia* and *2000 AD*. However, before we focus on particular texts, you will need to be familiar with the media terminology associated with magazines, to investigate briefly the state of the magazine industry and each title's position within it, to understand the ways in which magazines target and appeal to their audiences and the ways in which different audiences respond to different magazines.

Magazines come in a wide range of sub-genres which include lifestyle magazines, comics and online editions. To highlight their conventions and appeal, consider how they differ from newspapers. Magazine coverage is often more detailed but with less timely information. You are more likely to find features than hard news. Whilst a newspaper covers the day-to-day story, a magazine will explore and profile the issues and people involved. Magazines are weekly, fortnightly, or monthly while newspapers are daily and cover topics of general interest for a specific geographical area. Newspapers are ephemeral, but magazines are more permanent: we keep them for longer, re-read them and hand them on. Most importantly, magazines' content and audience are more specialised and focused. It's a bit like the difference between terrestrial and cable or satellite TV: mainstream channels have a broad audience but the cable channels are often more specialised, or niche. Magazine consumers appreciate information which is specifically aimed at their needs and interests.

You will need to familiarise yourself with the conventions of the magazine genre and to use the appropriate media terms. On the cover may appear: the title, the tagline, price, date of publication, main image with anchorage, possible straplines, sidebars or 'puff' trailing features or cover lines. Most magazines will have a contents page and editor's section, and most carry advertising. Magazines can also be divided into a number of different sub-genres.

Sub-genres
– smaller classes of a larger genre. For instance, hospital dramas and soaps are both sub-genres of TV drama.

'Magazines are printed and bound publications offering in-depth coverage of stories, often of a timeless nature. Their content may provide opinion and interpretation as well as advocacy. They are geared to a well-defined, specialised audience, and they are published regularly, with a consistent format.' (Johnson and Prijatel, 1999, p13)

TASK

In pairs, write down as many sub-genres of magazines you can think of, for example, 'hobbies'. Find out how supermarkets or newsagents like WH Smiths break them down into categories.

Analysing a magazine: the cover

A magazine's cover is its 'face'. While books are sold with only the spine showing except in only the largest shops, the magazine's cover is always on display. As with film posters or DVD covers, you can generally tell at a glance whether a magazine is for you. To understand how you make those judgements, consider a range of elements.

- The magazine's title: what connotations does it carry? *Nuts*, for instance, connotes craziness, but also crude masculinity. *Cosmopolitan* connotes someone who is at ease anywhere in the world.

- The strapline or tagline? These can be linked to brand identity / house style and to the title's values; and so to ideas about target audience. Is this magazine for 'men who should know better' or for 'women who juggle their lives'?

- The fonts and colours used. What do they suggest about the title's brand identity and target audience? Men's magazines like *Zoo*, for instance, frequently use a red, capitalised font, perhaps edged with black or gold to make it appear solid and bold; while teen girls' magazines like *Mizz* are more likely to employ pastel colours and round, 'friendly' fonts.

- The main image: often a woman gazing into camera. How femininity is represented, however, varies widely between sub-genres. On some covers, she may be sultry and alluring, showing lots of skin for the male gaze; while on others, she will be friendly, unintimidating and fully clothed. Masculinity, similarly, is represented in a range of ways, from Hollywood stars in sharp suits on *Esquire*, to the black and white image of an idealised unknown on the cover of *Men's Health*. Some titles favour 'pap shots' over airbrushed, studio-shot perfection, which tells you something about their genre, content and audience.

- The anchorage and cover lines – these will reveal a great deal about the title's ideologies and target audience. What kinds of story does this magazine cover? How do the mode of address and the given assumptions position the audience? Are they boy-mad, insecure schoolgirls, fit and financially solvent gay men, or politically aware ethical consumers of a certain age?

- Other tactics may range from the use of stars and celebrities, to sensationalism (count the exclamation marks!) and cover-mounted 'freebies'. How else does this magazine cover seek to persuade the consumer to buy?

TASK

Identify the house style of *Total Film*, *Grazia* and *2000 AD*:

- In what ways are the covers similar?

- How are they different?

Tagline
– a statement or catchy motto which captures the essence of a brand's identity. Magazines use taglines to offer clues about what they stand for, for example, 'for fun, fearless females!'

Strapline
– a secondary sentence attached to the magazine's name which says something about its brand image.

'House style' – relates to ideas about brand identity and mode of address. It provides continuity in language and is a term which describes a magazine's individual style and voice.

'Pap shots'
– photographs which have been opportunistically snatched by paparazzi, freelance photographers, usually of celebrities.

See Rayner et al.,
2004: pp.27–39
for a useful
chapter on image
analysis.

Analysing a magazine: between the covers

Now, look at the following:

- The contents pages – these offer not only an overview of the features but a sense of the title's brand identity through mode of address and design style. Are they formal and traditionally laid out; or chatty, image-led and colourful?

- The editor's letter – this is part of the magazine's brand identity and connection with its audience; a personal touch. What assumptions does it make about the intended audience?

- Two-page spreads – these are still the primary unit of design, but how are they laid out? Traditional grids work in a two or three column format and are formal looking and book-like, but a more edgy or modern title might use horizontal, modular lines as well as the traditional, vertical grid, sidebars, text wrapped around photos and images which bleed across the grid lines. Compare the design styles of three different magazines.

- The advertisements – given magazines' highly specialised audiences, the advertising they carry is also precisely targeted. Look at the proportion of advertisements to content and the kinds of brand which appear. What do they suggest about the target audience of the magazine you are analysing?

The magazine industry is generally dominated by major publishers, with a few notable exceptions like *The Big Issue* and *Private Eye*. Major magazine publishers include the following:

- IPC – American-owned and part of the biggest media conglomerate in the world, Time Warner, which also incorporates the internet provider AOL. Titles in its stable include *Now*, *Nuts*, *Sugar*, *Marie Claire*, *Loaded*, *NME*, *TV Times*, *Woman's Weekly*, *Pick Me Up* and *InStyle*.

- EMAP – previously a major player in the industry, but sold its magazine business to Bauer in December 2007.

- Bauer – a German company whose titles include *FHM*, *New Woman*, *Empire*, *Closer*, *Heat*, *More*, *Bella*, *Real*, *Spirit and Destiny*, *In the Know*, *Take a Break*, *That's Life* and *Grazia*.

- Condé Nast – in the UK, Condé Nast's titles include *Vogue*, *Easy Living*, *Glamour*, *Tatler*, *GQ* and *House and Garden*.

- The National Magazine Company (NatMags) – owned by Hearst, some of its titles are *Good Housekeeping*, *Cosmopolitan*, *She*, *Prima*, *Zest*, *Country Living*, *Esquire*, *Best*, *Reveal* and *Men's Health*.

- BBC magazines – a good example of commercial intertextuality or synergy. Many BBC magazine titles are spin-offs from successful shows, so they already have an established audience. They include the *Radio Times*, *Teletubbies* magazine, *Dr Who Adventures*, *Gardeners World*, *Top of the Pops* and *Top Gear*.

Many popular commercial magazine titles are global and are published in different countries. *FHM*, for instance, publishes 28 international editions and *Cosmopolitan* has 59 editions worldwide (hearst.com). This globalisation of the magazine industry suggests that magazine producers make stereotypical assumptions about their audiences. Mainstream, global titles like *Cosmopolitan* appear to target a homogenised audience and apparently assumes that those audiences all think the same way and want the same things, prominent cultural differences notwithstanding. However, most titles thrive by offering specialist subject matter to niche audiences.

The magazine audience is an increasingly fractionised one, with niche titles as obscure as *Trout and Salmon* or *Your Caravan and You*. Even within sub-genres the audiences are divided – for instance, *Kerrang!* targets a very different music fan than *Mixmag*. Magazine titles have a clearly defined and focused target audience. They target these audiences with a mode of address which 'speaks their language' and may contain preferred readings which their target audience is likely to agree with. This precisely defined readership enables publishers to 'sell' their audiences to advertisers who then buy space, which is how they make most of their money.

Until recently the magazine industry was generally characterised by increasing growth. In recent years, however, the industry appears to be doing less well and circulation figures for many titles, especially monthlies and teen girls' magazines, tell a worrying story for the industry. Felix Dennis, the previous publisher of *Maxim*, is quoted in *Economist* magazine as saying that 'it's a long, slow sunset for ink-on-paper magazines' (29 September 2007).

Nonetheless, competition remains fierce among the main publishers. New titles keep launching, and most of the growth is in the newer titles (with notable exceptions like *Cosmopolitan*). Magazines need to keep up-to-date with new technologies: most have websites and at least some of their content is available on mobile phone downloads.

Magazines are associated with 'me-time' and have a tactile quality and a portability which TV and computers struggle to match: they can be enjoyed in bed, in the bathroom or on the bus.

Synergy
– means 'working together' and refers to the way different arms of industry support and benefit one another. For example, a Warner Bros. film may use music from a band on a Warner Bros. record label, which will release the soundtrack CD/download.

ABCs – the Audit Bureau of Circulations audits the average circulation figures per issue of each magazine title over a six-month period. They also track whether sales are up or down, and so offers useful information to the industry about trends. This figure means that *Total Film* has sold, on average, 85,616 copies per issue over the last six months.

Total Film,

Future Publishing, £3.80 monthly. ABCs: 85,616

The issue referred to is March 08

Future Publishing was started on a kitchen table in Bath in 1985 and now publishes over 150 magazines worldwide. Its biggest are *Xbox 360*, *Total Film*, *T3*, *Official Playstation2*, *Digital Camera*, *Classic Rock*, *Total Guitar* and *Fast Car* (*The Guardian*, 30 November 2007). Future also holds the official licence for magazines from Microsoft, Sony, Disney and Nintendo to publish titles like *Official Nintendo Magazine*. These associations with new technology companies can be linked to ideas about target audience and synergy. Over 100 international editions of Future's magazines are published in 30 other countries around the world (http://www. futureus-inc.com/).

Total Film features reviews of new films but also celebrates old ones and countdowns of, for instance, 'the top one hundred Hollywood players' or 'cinema's saints and sinners'. The title has an extremely consistent format and layout. You will have noticed:

- On the cover – features which are indicated in the cover lines.

- Plus – the section on features which didn't make the cover.

- Buzz – film news and gossip.

- Lounge – home entertainment news and features.

- Every edition starts with a planner of the month's movie guide and a forum of readers' letters, and rounds off with quizzes and a film-related competition.

On the Future Publishing website, *Total Film* is described as 'vibrant, funny and accessible, mixing A-list glitz with indie attitude, instant hits with timeless classics'. Letters in the forum section are mostly from men and the advertisements *Total Film* carries appear to support the idea that the magazine is targeting a predominantly young, educated, male audience. Most advertisements support the film industry: DVD retailers Zavvi, HMV and Play feature frequently, along with adverts for games, gadgets, technology, occasional cars and beer, and pornographic phone lines tucked away at the back.

The mode of address in *Total Film* is playful, masculine and youthful: 'Indy Lego plot hunt!' is a feature which tries to work out the about-to-be-released *Kingdom of the Crystal Skull's* (2008) plot by looking at early shots of Lego's designs for the merchandise. The magazine manages to avoid being either too specialised or too 'laddish' in its mode of address by using a knowing, assertive yet informal tone. For example, the anchorage on film stills is frequently irreverent, funny and occasionally rude. In March 2008, anchorage on a very serious *There Will Be Blood* (2007) image of Academy Award winner Daniel Day-Lewis jokes that he is taking a moody puff on his cigarette to cover up the fact that he is picking his nose. *Total Film* clearly positions its audience as young, knowledgeable film lovers with a sense of humour.

The stereotypical representations of gender in *Total Film* reflect the gender bias in the mainstream Hollywood film industry. The magazine favours male actors and directors with talent and gravitas but does also include occasional interviews with (particularly attractive and sexy) actresses. For example, March 2008 features an interview with Katherine Heigl: 'I want to showcase my creativity... not just my bra size'. However, audience profiles for the magazine suggest that these stereotypical representations don't completely alienate female readers (it claims that 25% of its readers are women), perhaps because the magazine concerns itself with films rather than being a celebration of laddishness like a more traditional men's magazine such as *Zoo*.

Future Publishing sells this audience to advertisers in a range of ways. It claims that the average demographic is 75% male and is 26 years of age. The psychometric profile describes the *Total Film* readers as 'dedicated film-goers' who are 'first in the queue on the opening night' and 'love showing off their film knowledge to their mates' (http://www.future-advertising.co.uk/ads/portfolio/print.jsp?brand=18&print=30).

In your analysis of *Total Film*, you could also consider its use of stars and celebrities in magazines. Stars are manufactured by the industry: they are commodities. You might explore how and why stars and celebrities are used and this could be linked to ideas about star image. Richard Dyer suggests that star images are constructed and mediated identities, defined by their historical context and their culture. His approach considers how star images are formed by, and reflect, the ideology and belief systems of the society in which they are created. They are not only attractive and talented; they have to be culturally significant in some way.

Demographics – this approach to understanding the character of an audience makes generalisations about social groups. Demographic characteristics can be easily inferred, such as age, gender, ethnicity and educational level.

Psychometric profile – these profiles 'measure thought' and classify audiences by their values, attitudes and beliefs. This can also be linked to audience classification systems like Young and Rubicam's '4C's', originally from the field of advertising, which characterises consumers by their needs and values.

TASK

What does *Total Film*'s use of stars suggest about the symbiotic relationship between the magazine, the film industry, the stars themselves and the audience?

Stars are culturally significant because they represent shared cultural values and attitudes.

Symbiotic relationship – synergy in industry is a symbiotic relationship; different arms of the industry engender, rely on, support and benefit one another.

Grazia,

EMAP (Bauer), £1.90 weekly, ABCs: 227,083

The issue referred to is 11 February 2008.

Grazia was originally launched in Italy in 1938. Owned by Italy's market-leading publisher Mondadori, it's the number one weekly glossy in Italy and the UK. After an admittedly slow start in enticing high-end advertisers, *Grazia* now features glossy advertisements for D&G, Gucci, Louis Vuitton, Emporio Armani and a host of other designer brands. The 11 February 2008 edition carried 47 pages of ads across 149 pages.

EMAP Consumer Media (although *Grazia* is now owned by Bauer) spared no expense on the *Grazia* launch in Spring 2005. It spent £8 million in the first year and a total of £16 million in the first three years. Sales are increasing. The Audit Bureau of Circulations (ABC) reports that *Grazia* sells 227,083 copies over the counter each week – more than *Vogue* sells in a month. In volume, it sells more than the market leader, *Glamour*, with monthly ABCs of 550,066. But if *Grazia* is really read by 'upmarket' women as it claims, why does it charge much less for advertising (less than half) than other fashion magazines like *Glamour* or *Vogue*?

Grazia was arguably groundbreaking because it created a new 'news and shoes' generic mix. As Britain's first weekly glossy (up until *Grazia*'s launch they were all monthly), it combines glossy fashion with A-list celebrity gossip (referred to as interviews and lifestyle pieces) and elements of real life. *Grazia* stays up-to-date by being weekly at a time when weeklies are booming and monthlies are generally struggling. One of its taglines is 'a lot can happen in a week!'. It cleverly creates a hybrid mix of popular genres: it's contemporary in its fascination with celebrity but old-fashioned in the way it focuses on 'traditional' women's interests. *Observer Woman* suggests that *Grazia* is 'tapping the psyche of British women' (11 March 2007).

Grazia offers its readers narrative pleasures by constructing narratives about A-list celebrities: cover lines like *'Victoria to adopt baby girl?'* or *'Zahara's family want her back!'* use sensationalism or create enigmas. Narrative is constructed within the features, for example, in a story about a woman's 'personal journey' after her husband died when she was only 35. Narrative can also be identified in the familiar format and structure of the magazine, with its consistent design style and regular features. The before / after binary opposition can be found in the materialistic plugging of clothes and cosmetics: eyelash-defining mascara is apparently 'essential' and will change your life! Seasonal changes are also indicated and reflected in the fashions.

Grazia is more accessible to the average young woman who is interested in fashion than other fashion magazines because, in spite of its upscale brand image, it features clothes from high street staples Peacock and Primark as well as designer brands. The house style is gossipy, but includes some hard news features and a glossy, 'classy' mode of address which may suggest that *Grazia* has 'a higher percentage of ABC1 readers than any other woman's magazine except *Tatler* and *Harper's Bazaar*' (*Independent*, 21 August 2006). The cover image is frequently Victoria Beckham, although *Grazia* also favours actress Angelina Jolie and model Kate Moss.

TASK

Find the Bauer advertising rate card. How much does *Grazia* charge for a full colour page and how does this compare with *Heat* and *More*?

TASK

Compare an edition of *Grazia* with an edition of another woman's title like IPC's *Look*.

- What are the similarities and differences in house style and mode of address?

You could classify the *Grazia* audience in a range of ways. For example, with analysis of covers, features, advertisements and general design style, you could work out reader profiles (for instance, by looking at the extent to which ethnic minorities or people over 40 years of age are represented). Can we use Young and Rubicam's '4Cs' here and in what ways might the Uses and Gratifications model be useful in helping us understand why people read *Grazia*?

As you know, the Uses and Gratifications theory suggests that we use the media to gratify four main needs (see the earlier section on audience responses pg. 52). How might *Grazia* meet these needs for different audiences?

Cover lines
– appear on a magazine's cover. They announce features or relate to themes inside the magazine.

Sensationalism
– words and language used to provoke an emotional response from the reader.

Young and Rubicam worked in marketing and classified audiences in their '4Cs' consumer characterisation system by the needs that motivate and drive them. Look at http://www.4cs.yr.com/global/ to find out how Young and Rubicam stereotype audiences.

Intellectual property rights are covered by copyright laws and protect the ownership of ideas.

2000 AD,

£1.90 weekly, ABCs 20,000 approx.

The issue referred to is 23 January 08.

2000 AD emerged in the late-1970s, the era of punk sensibilities, when traditional children's comics like *Wizard* and *Hotspur* were losing readers. It was originally published by IPC / Fleetway, then Egmont, but is now owned and published by Rebellion, which owns intellectual property rights and is also well-known for developing computer games like *Alien vs. Predator. 2000 AD* is stable and growing, although only marginally profitable as a small part of a bigger industry which includes graphic novels and games. It carries very few advertisements: perhaps one for *2000 AD* merchandise and one for similar comics or videogames on the back page.

The genre of *2000 AD* is difficult to define because it has elements of a range of genres, including war, science fiction and action / adventure.

TASK

In what ways is a comic different from a magazine? Consider the following:

- The codes and conventions of comics such as framing, onomatopoeic sound effects and different shapes of speech bubble.

Hegemonic – hegemony has its roots in Marxist theory. It refers to the social and cultural control which the elite and privileged members of society have over their peers. A hegemonic view is that there are fundamental inequalities in power between social groups.

2000 AD features five different comic strips a week, with Judge Dredd the only constant fixture, while others like Strontium Dog come and go. While each story is self-contained to an extent, the strips are serialised within each 'prog' (issue) and often end with cliff-hangers.

Characters depicted are generally aggressive, macho, tongue-in-cheek, male and white. Settings are generally dark, post-apocalyptic, dystopian and futuristic, which links to the partly science fiction genre. We could arguably criticise *2000 AD* for violent content and the way it represents women. The absence of female characters in some editions could itself be considered a negative representation. The comic's ideology is hegemonic, although it positions the audience in contradictory ways. Characters aren't black and white and it can be difficult to know who to cheer for. The most violent character is a policeman (Judge Dredd), so *2000 AD* encourages readers to 'decode the various texts in complex ways and so form their own opinions on a variety of social and political issues' (http://medal.unn.ac.uk/casestudies/dredd.html).

It could be argued that *2000 AD* foreshadows trends with parody and political satire. Previous stories have included one about a show called *Sob Story* in *Mega City One* (Judge Dredd's post-apocalyptic home town) in which people moan and bewail their lives in the hope that viewers will give them money: predicting, perhaps, the recent popularity of 'reality' shows featuring people who will do pretty much anything for a bit of money or transient fame. Another strip in a previous edition, the 'Militant League of Fatties', parodied the idea of 'fat rights', although, of course, ultimately the militant fatties were too overweight to achieve much. This knowing, satirical tone may appeal to fans because it assumes that they have their own political opinions. Given the fluid and shifting nature of the preferred readings, *2000 AD* challenges its readers and is not just for children.

The fictional editor of *2000 AD* is Tharg the Mighty, whose customary greeting is 'The Mighty One speaks! Borag Thungg, Earthlets!' This idiosyncratic mode of address is part of the comic's appeal: understanding the language is one of the pleasures offered by the text and may encourage audience identification. 'Zarjaz', for instance, means good or cool. The comic contains many self-conscious in-jokes and intertextual references: in one strip, 'Kingdom', the heroic dog-soldier is called Gene the Hackman, after the American film actor. His foes are giant ants which he refers to as 'Them', in an intertextual link to the 1954 'creature feature' of the same name.

 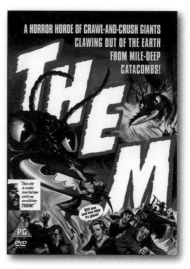

2000 AD fans are particularly loyal. The comic has its own fanzine, *Zarjaz*, and the average demographic of the *2000 AD* reader has aged alongside the comic itself.

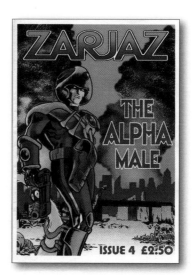

TASK

Look at a copy of *2000 AD*:

- Who is its primary target audience?

- How might this target audience be compared to that of *The Beano*? Compare an issue of each.

TASK

Investigating representations in *2000 AD*.

- With a focus on three specific strips or stories, compare the representations of heroism.

- Explain the representations of crime, law and the police in Judge Dredd.

EXTENDED TASK

- Explore the ways in which *2000 AD* reinforces or challenges typical representations of masculinity.

DC Comics is one of the largest and oldest comic books companies in the world. It brought us *Batman*, *Superman*, *Wonder Woman* and many more characters.

While *2000 AD*'s peculiarly British style and humour may exclude some international audiences, it is popular in the US, Australia and New Zealand – generally anywhere that English speakers can be found. DC Comics owns the North American publishing rights to *2000 AD*. It has spawned various films and computer games: not just *Judge Dredd* (1995), but a comic prequel to *Shaun of the Dead* (2004) appeared in prog. 1384 (April 2004) penned by the film's writers Simon Pegg and Edgar Wright. Rebellion has developed games like *Rogue Trooper* (Eidos), which won two BAFTAs and is based on a character from *2000 AD*. So *2000 AD* is a global brand.

Today *2000 AD* is less widely distributed than many other comics although it can be found in larger branches of supermarkets and WH Smiths. Back issues can be ordered online and they remain on sale at collectors' and fans' specialist shops, instead of being taken off sale and returned to the distributor like most periodical magazines. When a new edition of *Total Film* or *Grazia* comes on sale, the old ones are destroyed or returned and the retailer only has to pay for the copies sold. *2000 AD* will stay on sale even if it is an older issue because it is a collector's item. *2000 AD*'s cult status and relatively small circulation mean that traditional marketing methods are not necessarily the most efficient. These days it is mostly marketed on the internet and by word of mouth, due to its peculiarly loyal and long-lived readership, although Rebellion also attends comic and film conventions.

'Moral Panics' – in the media they stem from the idea that elements of popular culture can be blamed for wider problems in society; for example, we see computer games like *Grand Theft Auto IV* being blamed for violence and youth crime. They are cyclical in nature: concerns about the issue are raised in the media and reinforced by further coverage until 'action' is taken to curb the 'problem'.

Conclusion

Since magazines became popular more than a hundred years ago – thanks to increased leisure time among a growing literate middle-class, cheaper printing technology, electric light and better distribution – they have often been scapegoated as inferior elements of popular culture. The moral panics about the 'penny dreadfuls' in the Victorian era and the violent horror comics in the 1940s and 1950s can be linked to these debates about popular culture and the intrinsic worth or value of comics and magazines. The implication is that the content of comics like *2000 AD* may have a detrimental effect on audiences. While it is difficult to either validate or refute these suggestions, you may have learned from your own studies that audiences are able to negotiate their own understandings and decipher their own meanings from media texts.

SUMMARY TASK

Consider all three of the magazines discussed in this section. How do they market and promote themselves in different ways? You might like to consider the following:

- Launches.
- Marketing and advertising.
- Press and media packs.
- Giveaways and competitions.
- Mobile services.
- Subscription offers.
- Websites and fan sites.
- Conventions.

How do your chosen texts attract their audiences?

Bibliography

Books

Alden,C (ed.) (2007) Media Directory, *Guardian* Newspapers Ltd.

Branston, G. and Stafford, R. (2006), The Media Student's Book, 4th edition, Routledge: London.

Burton, G. (1990), More than Meets the Eye, Edward Arnold: London.

Helsby, W. (2004) *Children's Comics: A Teacher's Guide*, Auteur: Leighton Buzzard

Johnson, S and Prijatel, P. (1999) *The Magazine from Cover to Cover*, NTC Publishing Group

O'Sullivan, D. and Rayner, P. (2003), Studying the Media, 3rd edition, Arnold: London.

On the web

Audit Bureaux of Circulations: http://www.abc.org.uk/

National Readership Survey: http://www.nrs.co.uk/

Press Complaints Commission: http://www.pcc.org.uk/

Total Film website: http://www.totalfilm.com/

Total Film on Wikipedia: http://en.wikipedia.org/wiki/Total_Film

Grazia on Wikipedia:http://en.wikipedia.org/wiki/Grazia

2000 AD on Wikipedia: http://en.wikipedia.org/wiki/2000_AD_%28comic%29

www.magforum.com (useful profiles of UK publishers and their titles)

www.natmags.co.uk (useful core reader and brand profiles)

Further references:

Economist magazine September 29th, 2007

http://www.hearst.com/magazines/

http://www.futureus-inc.com/archives/2005/09/official_xbox_m.php

http://www.future-advertising.co.uk/ads/portfolio/print.jsp?brand=18&print=30

http://coverawards.com/tag/grazia/

Young and Rubicam's 4Cs: http://www.4cs.yr.com/global/default.asp?tid=b0c57e2f-6b8f-4e32-8b20-5bcf74124349

Charlton, M. Let the Punishment Fit The Crime: Evaluating Judge Dredd http://medal.unn.ac.uk/casestudies/dredd.htm Accessed 4/6/08

Advertising

Wendy Helsby

In this section you will:

- Closely study an advertisement for Chanel No. 5, concentrating on the areas of text (genre, narrative and representation), industry and audience.

- Consider the use of celebrity in advertising.

- Consider advertising regulation and the impact of controversial advertising through an exploration of a Dolce and Gabbana advert.

Advertising is the engine house for commercial media. It provides the income to sustain broadcasters, magazine publishers, radio and all the new communication technologies. Producers see adverts as giving audiences information about products and services, and therefore providing them with choice. But choice is difficult to manage and audiences are influenced by many factors, so the role of advertising is to try to target and deliver the audience to producers by converting the message conveyed in the advertising campaign into action – be it a change of attitude, a change of behaviour or a purchase.

TASK

In a small group, collect a range of adverts for different products; for example, perfume, cars and mobile phones. Try to get both print adverts and film or television adverts.

- Look at them carefully and then put them into categories according to their line of appeal for an audience – for example, sexual attraction, the independent woman, the successful businessman, the trendy teenager.

- How do the adverts group themselves?

- Are there similarities in the design of the adverts or their use of genre?

- Are there similarities in their use of conventions/style or narrative techniques?

- What can you say about the different ways in which these products target their audiences?

EXTENSION TASK

Choose one of the products from this task and investigate their advertising campaigns in more depth.

Consider the following points:

- Genre and appeal.

- Narrative themes.

- Gender representations and context.

- Audiences targeting.

- Producers and market positioning.

- Was an advertising agency used? Which?

- Regulations that might have influence, content or placement.

After you have completed your research prepare a short presentation on your selected campaign.

Chanel No. 5

The referenced advertisement can be viewed on www.YouTube.com alongside the 'making of' with commentary, released in 2004.

Background

Many established actors and directors have been lured into advertising campaigns and Chanel has been a regular user of star status to sell its products. After the success of *Moulin Rouge* (2001) Chanel brought the winning combination of Nicole Kidman (star) and Baz Luhrmann (director) to the campaign for its upmarket perfume, Chanel No. 5. They were knowingly using the link between the genre-star-director – and the audiences' knowledge of this intertextuality – in the hope of

Brand – a unique and identifiable symbol, association, name or trade mark which serves to differentiate competing products or services. Both a physical and emotional trigger to create a relationship between consumers and the product / service. (allaboutbrands. com)

Brand identity – a unique set of associations that the brand strategist aspires to create or maintain. These associations represent what the brand should stand for and imply a potential to customers. (allaboutbrands. com))

Brand image – a unique set of associations within the minds of the target customers which represent what the brand currently stands for and implies the current promise to customers. (Brand image is what is currently in the minds of consumers, whereas brand identity is aspirational.) (allaboutbrands. com))

capitalising on the film's success and the glamour of the star. Chanel claimed that the result was a 'creative first: the film to revolutionise advertising' (Chanel website). Globally its 'premiere' was even preceded by its own advertising campaign and in the UK it was even included in Channel 4 listings to help create a greater impression of an 'event':

'This is No 5: The Film, a three-minute movie or the world's most expensive advertisement, depending on your stance... The film to revolutionise advertising.' (*Sunday Telegraph*, article by Charlotte Edwardes 22 November 2004)

At £18 million, it is certainly a first in terms of budget. Kidman's £2 million fee alone is equal to the *entire cost* of the Oscar-nominated 1995 film *Trainspotting*.

Although principal photography was completed in five days in Sydney, Australia, *No 5: The Film* took 'many more months to complete' (Charlotte Edwardes, *Sunday Telegraph*, 22 November 2004).

An advert – whether costing millions like this and with a global name or for a local market – is made up of technical codes such as composition, lighting, colour, camera, *mise-en-scène*, sound and graphics. These combine with genre and narrative conventions and symbolic, social and cultural codes (to use Barthes' terms), to construct a line of appeal and to deliver messages about the **brand** image.

Genre

This is the unrequited love story, a 'brief encounter'. It mixes the loss of love based on stories like *The Lady of the Camellias* (Alexandre Dumas, 1852) and *Moulin Rouge* (2001) with the more optimistic theme of films like *Notting Hill* (1999), that inside every celebrity there is an ordinary person (in this case a dancer to reference the *Moulin Rouge* character) who could fall in love with an ordinary person whom they meet by chance. The generic conventions – of 'love at first sight', the barriers to love, the memories of love, doing one's duty (as with the endings of *Casablanca* (1942) and *Brief Encounter* (1945)) – are all encapsulated in this advert. The kiss is a central code to this genre, but, as a romance, sex is not. There is the fairy story theme that every woman would want to find their 'prince' even if he is a pauper! Like Cinderella, the ball gown becomes an ordinary outfit in a magical flourish using the appeal to magic solutions, which Judith Williamson (1978) refers to; but there is a twist to this in that this does not hinder romance but allows it to flourish. Chanel had based a previous advert on another fairy story, that of Red Riding Hood, so these references to the fairy story subtly link the two campaigns together.

Narrative

As with all stories, a series of enigmas and answers help to move the narrative forward. The key enigmas to be resolved are:

- Where can you find real love?

- Should you abandon career for love?

As the narrative unfolds this is answered through micro questions such as: Who is she? (We find out – 'the most famous…'.) Who is she running from? (We see the paparazzi… and so on.) The non-diegetic male voice-over helps to tell the narrative from the point-of-view of the male hero and so positions our identification with both the protagonists. Time and space are rapidly changed as we move from the streets of New York to a garret rooftop and back to the red carpet. These are similar to locations and *mise-en-scène* seen in *Moulin Rouge*.

The advert opens with the initial equilibrium of the hounded celebrity. The montage editing, monochrome colour and unusual camera angles connote her flight. The disruption is that in running away from the paparazzi she enters a taxi where she finds a young intellectual (he's reading!) who does not recognise her because he is so engrossed in his books. She escapes, says 'drive' and they have a brief affair in which she leaves the trappings of celebrity to be an ordinary girl. Then she is told by her controlling impresario / secretary (father role) and by her lover that her responsibility is to her public. She accepts her fate and returns to the red carpet. The new equilibrium is that she is now in control of her fame she always has the memory of that moment of escape, that 'brief encounter', to remember. She looks back to see the Chanel sign on the roof-top with the young man hanging off the crescent moon shape. The camera zooms in to a close-up of the jewel hanging down her bare back, a (diamond) ring with the logo No. 5 inside. The backward glance over the shoulder conveys the impression that even a film star is accessible.

The ideological message conveyed in the advert is that love is possible however seemingly unlikely the circumstance. This fleeting moment will be remembered through 'her kiss; her smile; her perfume'. The message is also that everyone has responsibilities and that sometimes sacrifice is necessary in order to meet them. This line of appeal is apparent through the mode of address. The binary oppositions which help to convey these meanings and resolve the fictional narrative are based on:

- Being out of – or in – control.
- The conflict between personal and public life.
- The differences between rich and poor.
- Being a celebrity or an ordinary person, the conflict between duty or emotion.

The dominant beliefs (ideologies) that are (re)established are those of duty and responsibility but also that, for the working woman, a career, glamour and romance are possible. But are these resolutions based in reality?

Representation

The Kidman character moves though three representations. Firstly, the hounded beautiful, female celebrity / star, conveyed through an extravagant stereotypically pink flounce dress with hair dishevelled as she runs, signifying how far she is out of control of her status as 'the most famous'. The stereotype is created by the blonde hair and the pink dress, again referencing *Moulin Rouge*, a sort of Disney Cinderella look. It is a classic stereotype and would be easily recognised by the audience. It is still a powerful image, nonetheless, one seen countless times in media texts. This creates a certain ambiguity for the reader. Second, the star is transformed by wearing an ordinary black and white suit when, as a 'dancer', she falls for the young man in the love scene on the rooftop. Finally she is seen in a black fitted gown, sleek and strong with hair pulled back and controlled as she moves calmly up the red stair case in front of the paparazzi, calmly accepting her destiny. Lighting helps to establish these changes. Starting from high key lighting with the paparazzi, we move to low key romantic lighting on the roof-top and the darkly lit space when she is told by her (male) lover and by her (male) secretary to return to the 'real' world; and finally to the spot lighting of the star on the staircase.

The young impoverished lover, Rodrigo Santono, reads, stereotypically wearing glasses connoting intelligence, unworldliness and naïveté (he is unaware of her fame). He is attractive, muscular, but ordinary. His clothes, such as the white vest, suggest this. The impresario / secretary in control of the star persona is a male, older, shadowy figure. He stands formally dressed in the background.

Representation of place

A New York cityscape is seen as a romantic, glittering city. The yellow cabs and the architecture immediately convey a sense of place. The swirling cameras, fast editing and bustle signify the energy of the centre of the celebrity world. Fireworks signify emotion and celebration. There are references to the *mise-en-scène* of the Paris seen in *Moulin Rouge* particularly with the roof-top scenes. The French connection of Moulin Rouge is additionally referenced by the romantic sounds of the non-diegetic music, Debussy's *Claire de Lune*.

Audiences

This advert is primarily targeting a young, reasonably up-market audience. The line of appeal is that romance will overcome differences. The brand image is of exclusivity but its re-positioning for the young is that this does not deny romance. The company's logo of two intertwined Cs is identified with the message throughout the advert. In the UK the advert was shown in cinemas and on Channel 4 targeting the young and alternative viewers of the channel as well as cinema audiences for films like *Moulin Rouge*. Viewers would have experienced the pleasure of recognising the intertextual references to *Moulin Rouge* as many of the scenes referenced this in their design through the *mise-en-scène* and in the cinematography. This pleasure is consciously exploited by the advert in a knowing way. The genre and narrative of lost love may also have appealed to an older audience, with possible connections to texts such as the voice-over in David Lean's *Brief Encounter*. The element of the man making the decision for the woman may also have linked with dominant ideologies of gender roles and appealed to male purchasers. In a simple way, therefore, this advert demonstrates how genders may respond differently to a particular narrative.

Identification for females would be with the glamour and status of the celebrity both in the advert and with Kidman herself. For young men it is with the lover, handsome, strong, a South American romantic who captures the heart of this star. He is the narrator and we follow his desire. For both primary and secondary audiences buying Chanel No. 5 would buy into this romantic dream or myth.

For audiences, the intertextual references in terms of the theme of lost love, the *mise-en-scène*, the cultural knowledge of celebrity, Kidman as star, but also the knowledge of other stars such as Marilyn Monroe (the icon of the paparazzi hunted and haunted star) would add to their engagement with the advert. Before she became a star Marilyn Monroe had been pictured nude across a red draped background for a calendar and had famously claimed in 1954 that all she had on when she went to bed was 'a couple of drops of Chanel No. 5'.

Industry

This advert is part of Chanel's ongoing high-profile campaigns linking celebrities to their brand image. It appeared in television schedules and was even featured on news programmes when first broadcast. Campaigns like this have to build upon previous messages (the previous campaign had been based on the story of Little Red Riding Hood and was a two-minute film). Much research will be undertaken by the advertising agencies involved to make sure that each new campaign reinforces, but also changes or updates, the message for the target audience to keep it contemporary, and particularly if the product changes or wants to reposition itself in the market place as Chanel wanted to do in this instance.

This campaign aimed to bring down the age of the purchaser of Chanel No. 5 which was seen to have gained an old-fashioned image. Previously, people who bought it were characterised as middle-aged men choosing it for their mistresses at airport shops or as a birthday present for their grandmothers. Chanel needed to revitalise the brand by getting young men to purchase it for their partners and for young women to wear it.

TASK

Discuss how linking the perfume with the film *Moulin Rouge* helps to lower its target audience age profile.

The advert itself was in fact a 'media event'. It was accompanied by a 25-minute film of 'the making of...' and when screened in cinemas had rolling credits at the end in order to help signify its filmic credibility. Interestingly, although the No. 5 logo appears a number of times the perfume bottle never appears, which again helped to position it as a film rather than an advert. Why would this be seen to be important? Is it that showing the bottle – the product – would have broken the fairy story spell?

Below you can see one of the display adverts that appeared with the movie campaign. There are obvious visual references to the film but the significant difference is the position of the bottle and the brand name. This identifies it as an advert first and foremost. Magazines have quite strict rules about what appears as an advert and what appears as editorial material. Without the bottle the advert might appear to be an image based upon a feature story around Nicole Kidman.

Chanel No.5 display ad

TASK

Consider how Nicole Kidman – actress, star, wife, mother, 'celebrity' – reflects the image of Chanel.

Although we do not generally think of adverts belonging to their own genres, perfume adverts such as Chanel No. 5 can be sub-divided into sub-genres and this shows how far discourses create meanings; in this case the discourses of romance and celebrity. Many contemporary adverts use celebrities which reflect upon the way celebrity is represented in the media. With perfume adverts, celebrity promises fame and romance. The use of celebrity endorsement is not new. Film stars such as Barbara Stanwyck, Debbie Reynolds and Marilyn Munroe all appeared in adverts for Lustre-Crème shampoo in the 1950s to connote glamour. Chanel is part of this genre of celebrity adverts, but you may have noticed how a particular sub-genre of the perfume / celebrity advert has been developing recently.

TASK

Look at the advert below. Although this is a print advert can you see similarities in terms of the conventions it uses with the Chanel advert?

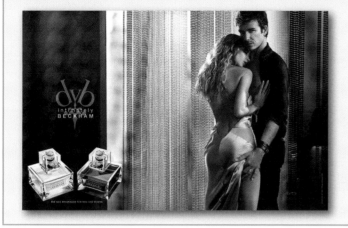

The advert is targeted at both women and men and is typical of perfume adverts where the people in the advert tend to personify the bottle of perfume. What you are buying here are bottles that are selling dreams, desires and aspirations.

How is this achieved?

The advert is divided into two with the dark borders framing a lighter central section where our focus goes first; the background re-emphasises the pale / dark binary opposition of the people. The bottles are laid out on the left border in a V shape reflecting the graphics above them. The graphics contain the initials of David and Victoria Beckham with the V given a feminine drape and below the words 'intimately Beckham'. Their lay out is reflected in the 'intimate' position of the people, so emphasising the link and the transfer of connotative meaning between bottles and people. The pale bottle is personified by the pale blonde female image with her dress a similar colour to the bottle and her hair to the bottle top, with the drape of her dress reflecting the V. The darker one is reflected by the darker male image. The man looks at us a direct and active mode of address whereas the female passively clings to the man.

The female wears a revealing evening dress, with bare back and leg, suggesting sexual availability. The man however is fully clothed; he is in control, his watch band stands out as an icon of masculinity. He is wearing a ring on his wedding finger connoting a relationship and is suggestively –' intimately' – holding the woman's leg. We buy into this intimacy. The iconic levels of denotation and connotation refer to the images of two famous celebrities. There is intertextuality in the form of the personas developed by the Beckhams. Cultural knowledge allows us to read the text and to take the underlying message about relationships and success in the shape of celebrity being available in the bottle. There are many similarities to the Chanel advert.

The Michael Jordan 1988 advert led to the banning of the black and red shoes in basketball and soaring sales of the Nike shoes. The black, red and white shoes symbolised 'hope, fame, money, success, enlightenment' for the black community.

As with the Chanel advert, this provides a 'mythic' message which we are being sold.

But what *is* being sold here? Do you find out how the contents of the bottles smell? What quantity are you buying? How much does it cost? Where to buy it? The 'myth' is that the perfume can give you the glamour of a beautiful woman or a strong masculine sexuality but with tenderness; in other words, a relationship like the Beckham's. It is carefully constructed not to send the wrong messages, particularly to men. This is not about androgyny CK-style, nor is it directed toward David Beckham's gay fan base. This is about getting female attention if you smell good.

TASK

Look back at how the advert is constructed and answer the questions:

- Does the advert reflect contemporary gender relationships?
- Do you have a different reading to the one above?
- Do you think this advert provides positive roles?

Try to explain your points-of-view clearly.

The 'Swoosh' and global branding – 'To the Next Level'

Although David Beckham wears Nike as a professional footballer, he does not (currently) endorse it as a brand. Given Beckham's global celebrity status it is an interesting point to consider – why doesn't he? The answer may lie in the brand image and brand identity of Nike.

Nike's 'swoosh' is one of the most recognisable global sports logos. Nike's image is based on urban 'edginess' and the company often uses renowned sports personalities who have had a 'bad boy' image, such as Eric Cantona and, lately, Wayne Rooney, or popular but non-mainstream activities such as break dancing.

In America, Nike's message often appeals to a particular ethnic group and its advertising campaigns focus on black athletes and the sports to which the black audience has an affinity, such as basketball.

Recently, in order to broaden its appeal to other audiences, Nike has also moved into areas such as the female market through street dancing. (These adverts can be viewed on www.youTube.com.)

A study of Nike raises questions about globalisation and about cultural and global imperialism. When you go to buy locally (in the UK, for example) are you really buying globally? What else have you bought apart from a pair of trainers or a T-shirt? Have you, perhaps, bought in to a global fashion trend or contributed to global homogenisation? Nike, it appears, understands this global / local contradiction and, with its global campaigns such as the recent (April 2008) football campaign 'To the Next Level' (a two-minute film directed by Guy Ritchie of *Lock, Stock and Two Smoking Barrels* (1998) broadcast during the 2008 European Football Championships), it has referenced the local; Ritchie's global video is given a regional (local) feel by focusing on particular footballers depending on the continent from which you are viewing. The advert combines scenes on the football pitch with off-pitch glamorous nightlife and crass (male) humour, such as 'mooning'. The narrative subject, from whose point-of-view the game is 'played' is the viewer who 'plays' for a Premiership club against the world's greatest footballers, such as Ronaldo. The edgy style links with the edgy urban nature of previous campaigns and also offers intertextual reference to Ritchie's black comedy gangster movies.

The campaign, like other Nike ads, was globally released on television and online on the Nike website. It also provided interactivity as you could sign up for a training programme, allowing the viewer to become more deeply engaged in the Nike message. In 2008 Nike also released adverts for the Olympics in Beijing made specifically for Chinese audiences. These show ordinary Chinese citizens suddenly performing extraordinary athletic feats (www.altogetherdigital.com/20071002/chinese-olympics-adverts-from-nike/).

Such local advertising suggests that Nike is aiming to provide a local message on a global sale.

But, who benefits?

Sport is a commercial and cultural global industry and the advertising 'job' is to promote it and to commodify the aspirations and inspiration sport provides. Nike hopes the world will buy into this commodification by purchasing the Nike logo and the Nike message of grass roots sport. In sport advertising it is possible to see how power and representations are reflected through the adverts and how this in turn is influenced by globalisation of sport. The debate raised is how far global imperialism, the trans-national control by a few conglomerates, imposes identities onto local cultures; or how far there is an exchange of ideas through the ability of the global economy to reach local consumers and react to their needs so that cultural imperialism is not a wholly one-way process?

Nike's base is in the USA but it has relatively few employees there; the production is done by workers in factories in countries like Indonesia. Interestingly the co-

Further discussion on globalisation can be read at www.mediaknowall.com/advertising/globalad and in Hesmondhalgh, 2006.

For further information the ASA website can be found at www. asa.org.uk. and OFCOM at www. ofcom.org.uk

founder of the company (Phil Knight) stated that the 'three-legged stool' of Nike's success consists of celebrity endorsement, product design and advertising (Hatfield, *The Guardian*, 17 June 2003). Efficient economic production is omitted from this metaphorical stool and Nike has been frequently criticised for the exploitation of developing world workers particularly those in the Far East. Whatever the outcome of these debates, one fact in undeniable: the majority of the profit is bound for American shores and this economic control could be regarded as the clearest form of global and cultural imperialism.

Regulation and advertising: violence, sex and the vulnerable

The advertising regulator in Britain is the Advertising Standards Authority (ASA). It started in the 1960s regulating print advertisement whilst, at the time, broadcasting had its own regulatory authorities. Since 2003, however, the ASA has worked under the auspices of Ofcom and is now responsible for regulating **all** advertisements. The ASA uses the CAP code (Code of Advertising, Sales Promotion and Direct Marketing) against which it adjudicates complaints received about advertisements.

An advert has to deliver its message in a brief moment as a reader flicks through a magazine or watches it on screen. This encourages the use of shorthand cultural references and often with this comes the use of stereotypes. However, audiences are not homogenous and even if some of the target, primary and secondary audiences take the message as intended, others may not. And, as you already know, media texts are often polysemic and adverts are no exception. So there is sometimes a problem for producers because they cannot guarantee that audiences will read adverts in the preferred way. It is rarely the intention of the advertiser to cause offence or to misguide audiences (although some advertisers actively attempt to stir up controversy). If they do and the adverts end up causing offence then the regulators may become involved.

Look at the advertisement below for fashion house Dolce and Gabbana.

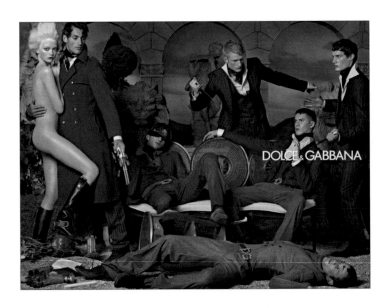

In what ways might different audiences read this advert?

This advert shows a scene in which the clothes are being worn in a stylised composition against a backdrop of classical archways and landscape referencing the genre of historical paintings. The monochrome nature of the advert adds to this artistic language. The clothes on the young men are shades of greys and blacks, whilst the young woman to the left stands out in her flesh-coloured nakedness and blonde / whitish hair. A female nude is often seen in classical paintings, but this one wears fashion boots. A revenge tragedy appears to be played out in the genre further emphasising the style of historical classical paintings. One man wearing a great coat, again connoting the (fashionable) past, holds a gun whilst another brandishes a knife.

This image was part of a campaign for the up-market brand of clothes targeting an affluent market, one which might be expected to recognise the intertextual references to particular paintings. However, the ASA received a comparatively large number (166) of complaints about this campaign. An explanation for this may be the contemporary context as there was a debate over gun and knife crimes in the media when the advert first appeared in Jan 2007. The complainants felt that the campaign, with its glamorised images, was irresponsible and appeared to condone violent crime. Dolce and Gabbana replied that it was inspired by well known paintings of the Napoleonic period and their stylised nature did not suggest aggression or condone violence. However:

'The ASA disagreed and upheld the complaints. It considered that the first ad showed the knives being brandished aggressively and gave an overall impression of violence. As a result the ASA ruled that the ads could be seen as condoning or glorifying knife-related violence and were therefore irresponsible and likely to cause serious or widespread offence' (www.asa.org.uk/asa/adjudications/Public/TF_ADJ_42118.htm, Dolce & Gabbana).

It might well have been the case that without the topical concern about young men and knife culture in the UK, this advert would have not attracted as many complaints as it did.

TASK

Look at other Dolce and Gabbana adverts. Consider the ways in which the characters have been represented. How might different audiences interpret these adverts?

Conclusion

Advertising works on audiences in many ways through lines of appeal such as fear and one-up-man-ship, psychologically and socially. Judith Williamson (1978) talks about advertising selling us ourselves; in other words we buy into our self-image that we see in the advert. Producers deliver these messages through adverts which contain meanings, ideas, values and beliefs. They use a wide range of platforms, global as well as local, which increasingly have meant their target audiences are more diffuse than mass. The advantage of the web and the blogosphere is that it provides a free media buzz. Consider the story of the Dove Campaign for Beauty, where Dove has introduced a dialogue between its consumers on the definition of beauty. 'The Real Truth About Beauty' is shown in the advert 'Dove Evolution' where an ordinary female face is manicured and then digitally enhanced to create a 'perfect' image finishing with the tagline 'No wonder our perception of beauty is distorted'. This has been viewed on YouTube by millions of people. (Dove is owned by Unilever and at an economic level this advert was risky.)

The power behind these mass media messages is in the hands of a relatively small group of producers, although the potential of the web suggests that another model of 'bottom-up' advertising may be possible. The *Dove* evolution campaign, for example, was parodied by a 'slob evolution' response where a good looking man was converted into a slob. Like other industries in this brave new media world much is uncertain. How far will the new technologies and changing economic structures change the world of advertising?

Once people and companies have things to sell advertising is inevitable. How far it controls, or is controlled by, us the consumers and by those who produce adverts reamins a major question in Media Studies.

Bibliography

On the Web

www.screenonline.org.uk – a fantastic site for background into advertising on British television and film. Also has classic clips to view such as the tombstone AIDS campaign advertisement.

www.paintedcows.com/international – this is a website that will lead you to many other national sites and discusses both national and international issues in advertising and marketing.

www.ipcmedia.com – magazine media packs includes *Nuts*, *Loaded*, *Uncut*, *NME*.

www.warc.com – World Advertising Research Center. This is a subscription website for professionals in the media, marketing and advertising but it does have a free trial. www.asa.org.uk – Advertising Standards Authority. Find out about the CAP code and adjudications; it has an excellent college / schools site with downloadable material.

www.mediamagazine.org – excellent resource with case studies on campaigns written with A level students in mind. Can access archives if a subscriber to the magazine.

Dugdale. H. 'Product Placement and the Fast Forward Generation', www.mediamagazine.org, September 2006

Dugdale, H. 'Goodbye Mr Linekar', www.mediamagazine,org Number 18, September 2007

www.mediaknowall.com – good resource for clear explanations of key concepts such as media effects and good links.

www.YouTube.com – where you can find video clips of television and film adverts.

In addition the websites of specific companies provide ample material for researching campaigns.

Books

Armstrong, K. (1999), Nike's Communication with Black Audiences. A Sociological Analysis of Advertising Effectiveness via Symbolic Interactionism,' in *Journal of Sport and Social Capital* Vol 23, No 3 266-86

Cook, Guy (1992), *The Discourse of Advertising*: Routledge: London and New York

Curran, J., Collins, R., N. Garnham, P. Scannell and P. Wingate (eds) (1986), *Media, Culture and Society: A Critical Reader*, London: Sage

Davies, Jim (1998), *The Book of Guinness Advertising*, London: Guinness

Dyer, G. (1982), *Advertising as Communication*, London: Routledge

Dyer, R. (1985), 'Taking Popular Television Seriously' in David Lusted and Philip Drummond (eds) *TV and Schooling* London: BFI

Fiske, John (1982), *Introduction to Communication Studies*, London and New York: Routledge

Goffman, E. (1978), *Gender Advertisements*, Cambridge, MA: Harvard University Press

Gumbel, A. 'Boom in "brand integration" gives advertising the break it needs' in *The Independent* 5 November 2005

Habermas, J. (1989/1962), *The Structural Transformation of the Public Sphere* (trans. T. Burger and F. Lawrence), Cambridge: Polity

Hall, S. (1997), *Representation: Cultural Representations and Signifying Practices*, Thousand O Hatfield, S. 17th June 2003 'What makes Nike's advertising tick' *The Guardian*

Hesmondhalgh, D. (ed.) (2006), *Media Production* DA204 Understanding Media Course, Milton Keynes: Open University

Helsby, W. (2004), *Teaching TV Advertising*, Auteur: Leighton Buzzard

Jackson, S.J. Andrews, D.L. (eds) *Sport, Culture and Advertising: Identities, Commodities and the Politics of Representation*, London: Routledge

Leiss, William, Stephen Kline and Sut Jhally (1990) *Social Communication in Advertising*. London: Routledge

Mahmud, S. 'Nike takes Soccer to 'the Next Level' *Adweek* Online 1st May 2008

Monahan, Jerome 'TV sponsorship' 3rd Feb 2003 www.mediamagazine.org

Morley, David (1980), *The 'Nationwide' Audience: Structure and Decoding*, London: BFI

Williamson, J. (1978), *Decoding Advertisements: Ideology and Meaning in Advertising*, London: Marion Boyars

RESEARCHING, CREATING AND EVALUATIONG YOUR OWN MEDIA PRODUCTIONS

Researching, Creating and Evaluating Your Own Media Productions

Mandy Esseen & Pip Jones

Introduction

This final chapter deals with important aspects of the internally assessed elements of advanced level Media Studies, where you are likely to be required to undertake planning and production work. You might also be required to produce a research investigation which may then culminate in a production activity. Whatever you have to do – and here your teacher will guide you – you are almost certainly going to need to begin by undertaking some research. This may then develop into a pre-production (planning) activity like storyboarding, scripting or producing a mock-up and this in turn may lead on to a production; for example, creating a film trailer, a series of connected web pages or your own computer game. Finally, you will have to evaluate the work you have done in some form or another.

In this section you will:

- Be given ideas and suggestions about how to approach pre-production and production work in creative ways.

- Be offered advice on the best way to research and reference your work.

- Be shown how pre-production work links with and leads naturally on to production work.

- Be guided on how to manage group work.

- Find out how to set up focus groups and write questionnaires to get valuable audience feedback.

- Learn how to produce effective evaluative reports.

Pre-production Planning Activities

A working definition to help you decide on the types of pre-production pieces you could create might be: *work in progress which reflects research undertaken and takes into account an anticipated audience*. Your pre-production may take the form of plans, designs, drafts, scripts or storyboards.

You may be set a brief by your teacher or you may be given a wider choice. For example, you may have been studying trailers for different films and may have been asked to create the planning stages of a new science fiction film. Having grasped the key conventions of a film trailer, you may decide to create a storyboard for a new sci-fi film trailer or, alternatively, a DVD cover for the new film.

Sample brief

1. AN INDIVIDUAL PRE-PRODUCTION

Your task is to produce either:

1. A storyboard for the trailer of a new sci-fi film.

OR

2. To use your ideas for a new sci-fi film to produce the DVD cover for the film.

2. A PRODUCTION ASSIGNMENT

Your task is to produce either:

1. The trailer for ONE OF YOUR GROUP'S storyboards. You may work on this together but please plan and discuss your individual roles carefully before you begin.

OR

2 A series of posters (3) for your new film. THIS TASK MUST BE DONE INDIVIDUALLY.

3. A REPORT

This must be done individually. It should be between 1,200 – 1,600 words and should focus on:

a. The research you did to inform your pre-production.

b. A justification of the target audience for your production.

c. An evaluation of the production, highlighting strengths and weaknesses through a comparison with existing sci-fi trailers or posters.

The brief above, typical at AS level, outlines three separate pieces of work you will need to complete. Make sure you understand the requirements of all the parts before you begin. Read what is required for the report so that you know how to begin your work.

Storyboards can be hand-drawn or produced using a digital camera. Either way, you will need to have planned carefully what will appear on the screen and ensure that if you indicate a close-up (for example) under camera instruction, then this is reflected in the visuals. There are a number of different ways a storyboard can be constructed but for the purpose of your AS level Media Studies you will, at the very least, need to include the following information:

VISUALS, SHOT LENGTH, CAMERA INSTRUCTIONS AND SOUND TRACK DETAILS. Many students also like to include a 'comments' section for further explanations.

You must also make sure that you comment on the transitions between the frames – for example CUT or FADE or WIPE. A good web site to learn more about camera language is: http://www.mediaknowall.com/camangles.html.

Comment	
Sound Track	
Camera Instructions	
Visuals	
Shot Length	

Television and film scripts need to be accurately laid out and it is worth remembering that this is as – if not more – important than the quality of the drama itself because the layout and format of your script IS the pre-production activity. Look at the BBC Writers' Room web site at http://www.bbc.co.uk/writersroom/ scriptsmart/ for help on how to structure a television script.

Often specifications – and teachers – refer to MOCK-UPS in relation to print based pre-productions. Be careful here though – no one is asking you to produce a hastily drawn sketch! You may be asked to produce a mock-up for a CD cover, a series of advertisements or a magazine front cover and contents page. These need to be produced carefully using whatever DTP facilities you have available and using your own photographs. Advertising agency professionals presenting a mocked-up campaign to a client would not produce something that wasn't as close to a finished product as they could make it! The purpose of the mock-up is to show the client an almost finished product that they can comment on.

Production: making decisions

Before you throw yourself into hastily devised productions and research projects, take a moment to stop and think about why this type of work is important. It is an essential part of any advanced level Media course for many reasons:

- It offers you a chance to respond to the more theoretical aspects of your course in practical ways.

- It is a way for you to demonstrate your understanding of the relationship between texts, industries and audiences.

- It is a chance for you to produce your own media texts.

- It provides opportunities for you to be creative!

Whether you have a vague idea, a clear idea or no idea at all about what to create, you have choice available to you in terms of what you *could* create and so you need to begin by making a few key decisions:

- Have you been given a brief? Make sure you understand all of its parts.

- What equipment is available to you?

- Will you work on your own or as part of a group?

- Is there a clear link between your planning and / or research ideas and your production? Make sure you've talked this through with your teacher.

- Will you produce a mainstream, niche or alternative text? In other words are you going to replicate or challenge existing conventions? There is nothing to be gained by, for instance, subverting genre conventions or challenging masculine identities just to be different. If you are going to do this you need to think carefully about **why** as well as **how** and whether there is a viable market and audience for your product. Always be able to justify your decisions.

A Note About Group Work

You may decide to undertake a production as a group, but remember - group work is not always the easy option!

Check with your teacher on the specific guidelines for group work with your Awarding Body. These do vary – some allow group work only for video productions. You may be told that you can create a production at AS as a group piece, so long as you have produced individual pre-productions and write individual evaluations. At A2 level, however, the production may be linked to an individual investigation into an aspect of genre, narrative or representation. Consequently, if a group wished to make a production together at this level they would need to have discussed their investigations together FIRST so that each member would be able to contribute something to the production from their investigation.

For example, a group of three students who wanted to make a horror film for a teenage audience may well decide to investigate three separate areas relating to horror, for example: a) recent developments in horror genre, b) the use of narrative subversions in contemporary horror films and c) the representation of teenagers in selected horror films.

The group's production could then be a trailer for a new horror film which would incorporate elements of the research undertaken by each of the group's members.

A useful tip is to ensure that your group is not too big. Three is ideal, with four as a maximum. You need to ensure that each group member has a discrete task or area of responsibility. For example, you may decide to each take a scene and take total responsibility for it, or you could decide that one person will be the director, one will be responsible for the sound, lighting and camera and one will have overall responsibility for editing. Of course, you will help each other out but it is useful if you have clear areas of responsibility before you begin.

You will need to be meticulous in recording your own contribution and responsibilities throughout the process so that you can explain them in your evaluation. A really good tip here is to keep a diary / log of your choices (including elements you reject as well as those you include) so that when you write your evaluation you will have very specific details to include.

Clearly, planning for any production requires you to think about what you know already in order to think about what you still need to find out; and, obviously, with the media so convergent and inter-related, you also need to consider your target audience – perhaps in terms of their age, gender and lifestyle and how they may view, read or use the production.

To help you think about your audience you might like to begin by asking yourself what other kinds of text they might be consuming. For example, if you were publishing a niche film magazine, you may decide your target audience would be predominantly aspirational males, aged between 16 and 35 who enjoy using digital technology and 'gadgets'. They may well read magazines like *Empire*, graphic novels like *Sin City* and play games like *Tomb Raider*. They may enjoy being cast in the role of expert when discussing films and games with friends. Knowing that your target audience is likely to enjoy certain types of media product gives you the perfect starting point for your planning activity.

Look closely at the following chart which indicates the key characteristics of different types of text. You may wish to use this to help you decide on your pre-production and the expected style and finish of your productions. Notice the examples given of different types of text and spend some time thinking about *where* your text will be seen as well as by whom.

Comparing Different Types of Production

	PRODUCTION VALUES	TARGET AUDIENCES
MAINSTREAM For example, a celebrity general interest magazine with a focus on gossip, scandal, image and high profile exposure.	• High-budget magazines, films, TV programmes. • Glossy, high-quality paper or multi-cam, multi-take scenes. • Exotic locations. • Well-known stars / celebrities / directors / producers. • Subversions, if used, are well signposted and 'obvious.' • High sponsorship / advertising space / time to help cover costs.	• Wide range appeal to many different sectors of society. • Texts are often closed, with clear preferred meanings encoded encouraging a more unified response.
NICHE OR SPECIALIST For example, an educational computer game to help children improve their maths and number skills.	• Can be high-budget, but not always – this will affect the 'finish' of the production. • An emphasis on specialist knowledge and / or jargon to address audiences as 'expert'. • Subversions tend not to be used – the focus is on establishing a reinforcement of specialist trends and characteristics.	• Narrower audience. • Texts can be closed with clear preferred meanings drawn from a pre-determined set of responses to accepted and *specific* issues. • Use of jargon that audience understands helps it to feel sense of belonging.
ALTERNATIVE For example, a fan website or fanzine for an indie band.	• Usually low budget – may struggle with funding. • Little emphasis on production values – poor paper quality may be used; or hand held camera techniques. • An emphasis on breaking mainstream conventions and rules. • Experimental techniques used.	• Usually a narrow audience drawn to the originality and possibly experimentation of the open texts. • Enjoyment is gained from the subversion of rules. • Audiences are sophisticated and experienced at reading complex, multi-layered texts.

Consider the scope and appeal of each area and think carefully about the brief your teacher may have given you – or your own ideas. Do you want to create something which mimics or challenges accepted formats? Either approach is acceptable – but the decisions need to be yours.

Once you have made a decision on the type of product you are going to create, you could then look at some comparable products. For example, you may have decided to make your own niche magazine, so a good starting point would be to make a list of the conventions of the magazines you have studied and read. Include notes on, for example, how the pages are laid out, how images are used, the image:text ratios, the use of colour (especially at certain times of the year) – and the overall mode of address. Or you may be working on a task which requires you to create the DVD cover for a new horror film. Here, analysing comparable products and horror genre conventions would be sensible starting points. However, if your production task is to create a website or a double-page spread which promotes your horror film, you may also need to ask your target audience directly about their own preferences. To do so you may need to create and distribute a questionnaire in order to justify your target audience, investigate their preferences and then use this information to target them successfully. Here questionnaires are an effective research method.

Independent research is required throughout your Media Studies course – whether you are planning your AS coursework, reading up on theoretical issues or preparing for a more detailed A2 investigation.

Your AS research is likely to be straightforward and research into comparable products is likely to be your starting point but at A2 you may be asked to undertake an individual investigation into an area of genre, narrative or representation. You may have a free choice and could, for example, decide to investigate film texts, computer games or magazines. Take time to consider your options and to frame a workable question or hypothesis for yourself. You will need to consider how best to conduct your research and what different research methods may suit your investigation best.

However, it is worth remembering that research for its own sake is an interesting activity, you will need to be focused and selective about the research you do undertake. You need to be aware of the different research methods you *could* undertake to help you collect, collate and analyse the information you need to make your pre-productions and productions effective. Read the following section carefully but remember we are not suggesting that you use all these available research methods, only that you select the most appropriate for your own work.

Research Methods

These are divided into two types; primary research and secondary research. Primary research is first-hand information retrieved by the researcher and includes the following:

- Textual analysis.

- Content analysis.

- Questionnaires.

- Focus groups and interviews.

- Observational studies.

Secondary research refers to information that someone else has collected and often published. Useful sources include:

- Books.

- The internet.

- Newspapers.

- Television programmes.

- DVDs.

- Journals / magazines / periodicals.

You are likely to need to use a mixture of both primary and secondary methods to be able to explore, research and, perhaps, challenge ideas.

Deciding which methods will suit you best

The best way to 'learn how to do research is by actually doing it, but a great deal of time can be wasted and goodwill dissipated by inadequate preparation.' (Bell, Doing your Research Project, 2005, p1)

So, to help avoid wasting time and effort, the following points will help guide you in your initial approach:

1. **Identify the research you need to do for your selected topic** – for example, a pre-production task might require you to plan a draft design of a CD cover for a new band or artist while your production task might be to create a fan site for the band or a double page spread in a music magazine which promotes it. Here you might need to consider primary research into the genre conventions of CD covers or the representations of the artists, depending on your specific slant. You might also want to consider looking at the layout, codes and conventions of magazine pages.

   You may need to undertake research for a more formal essay-style investigation into an area of selected media output. Here it may be useful to base your research on an initial focus group. For example, you may decide to analyse the representation of women in selected advertisements, and so you may want to frame your research in the form of a question, for example: Do stereotypical images of women dominate contemporary advertisements? An investigation based on five current print adverts. For this task you could begin by undertaking some secondary research – reading some relevant books on gender representations and on decoding advertisements and then you might use this information to analyse your selected adverts before asking a sample of people for their responses to them.

2. **Be realistic** – this is particularly important in relation to a small-scale project because you don't want to take on too much. Students are often too ambitious and set themselves impossible tasks, which often result in failure, as they do not know how to make good use of all the information. So, for example, if you are researching representations of the family on television in preparation for an investigation, you may want to limit your research to two episodes from two contrasting programmes.

3. **Be objective** – this is perhaps one of the most difficult points to grasp, but at the same time one of the most important considerations in any research project. As a researcher you need to take a step back and examine the facts. Try to avoid the temptation to guess or assume things. By keeping an open mind you may well be surprised by what you find out.

Remember:

- Always choose a topic which interests you and then select a narrower area within that field to research. For example, you may be considering analysing representations of men in adverts. You might then limit your investigation to cosmetic or grooming products.

- Search for a range of texts that are relevant and then choose the ones you want to focus on, for example, Gillette and L'Oréal Men Expert.

- Find more examples of each campaign and notice how particular textual elements work in each one.

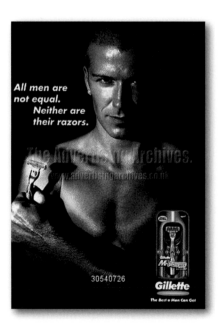

Approaching Your Research 1: secondary methods

The most common research strategies used by students are: reading books and internet articles to gain a more detailed insight into genre, narrative, representation and audience issues; analysing comparable products; and conducting audience research through questionnaires and focus groups. Consequently it is quite likely that you *will* begin your research with secondary research methods before moving on to the more 'hands-on' primary methods.

So it's a good idea to get to know your Learning Resource Centre (LRC) / Library and learn how to use it effectively. Here are some tips to ensure that you become effective researchers.

Books

Because of the Dewey Decimal System of Classification, books which will be useful in your research may not always appear under 'Media' in your library. By performing book searches, you will be able to access books not just from the Media and Film sections but also from other specialist areas. For example, many Psychology and Sociology books cover media-related issues, from audience effects to case studies on representation. If you are investigating crime, then law books may highlight media involvement and if you are looking at advertising then many Business Studies books are likely to yield excellent results.

The internet

The internet offers vast amounts of resources that are otherwise not available in any one geographical location. It is, quite literally, the biggest library in the world and so it is important that users know what information they actually need to find out. The results of random searches can be overwhelming and information found is not always relevant, accurate or even true.

The web is world-wide and does not have an owner. Censorship does not exist and you must bear this in mind. Anyone can post information so you need to be a critical user always looking for problems with the information that is being provided, as well as its beneficial points. You must try to assess the reliability of the information you are finding and to do this you need to be critical of it. Always ensure you check your sources and consider these points:

- Who has written the material?

- What is their level of knowledge and expertise?

- Is there any bias or vested interest?

- Has the information been sponsored? Who by? Are any implications attached to this?

Your initial searches may not be successful. Many students, when given a broad subject area, for example 'women' and 'horror films', will place these words into a search engine and will find that they have hit thousands of sites: every site that has

The Dewey Decimal System of Classification – the numbers and letters on the spines of books help to catalogue them into different categories. The system is based on 10 classes of subjects (000–999), which are then further sub-divided by using the metric system. The first part of the number is the main subject area – for example, media, 302 – and then after the decimal point the other numbers refer to the content within that book. Then three letters will follow, meaning the first three letter of the author's surname.

Top tip – use the indexes located at the back of the book to search for key words to help you find the pages that you need.

Most databases use 'Boolean operators' to help you control your search better by linking your keywords together. If you link women, horror and film with the Boolean term AND (women AND horror AND film), all three terms must be present in each of the documents found by the search. Another Boolean is OR, which can also help you to narrow your search.

the word 'women' and 'horror' and 'films' will come up. Hence the millions of hits found.

Here are some useful tips to make searching on the internet more productive and quicker:

- Try using Boolean operators.

- Use more search terms to get better results.

- Search for phrases by using quotation marks.

- If it's just British media that you are going to cover, limiting the search to British sites can help.

- There are search engines that can help you refine your search results. Search engines Hotbot and Google allow the user to perform an advanced search, which can even just find sites that have been updated in the last week, which is particularly good if you are regularly surfing.

- Experiment with different search engines if you are not successful with your usual choice – Altavista, Dogpile, MSN, Google, Hotbot and Yahoo are a few to consider.

Once you have found, read and synthesised your research information, it is time to develop your ideas and this is where primary research methods become important.

Approaching Your Research 2: primary methods

Textual analysis

A lot has already been said about textual analysis in this book and it would be a good idea to look back to Section 1 before you use textual analysis as a research method. Generally, it might be useful to use some basic semiotic approaches. As you know by now, semiotics is a study of the visual signs that help us to get meaning from a text. When we read a sign, the first stage is working out the denotation, the literal or common sense meaning of a sign. For example, a red rose is a flower and an apple is a fruit. The second stage is to consider the connotation (what it may suggest). For example, a red rose could mean love; or be a symbol of New Labour; or a symbol for those who live in Lancashire. The apple could represent New York; healthy living; or the Beatles. Meanings, as you can see, are dependent on context. Analysing comparable products, so you know how conventions are used, is an effective first stage in understanding the genre conventions of your own creative work.

Content analysis

This is a flexible research technique for analysing large bodies of text. It follows a clear set of steps and is a measured way of obtaining results. The task of content analysis is to examine a selected (sampled) number of texts, and to classify the content according to a number of pre-determined areas. For example, if you are researching gender bias in the filming of sports texts, you might count the number of close-ups on male and female players in five minutes of play at Wimbledon.

Questionnaires

Before you begin to design a questionnaire, you need to decide whether one questionnaire is necessary and will actually yield useful information and data. Consider these points before you begin:

- What exactly do you need to find out?
- Why do you need to know this?
- What are you hoping to explore, prove or disprove?
- Exactly what questions do you need to ask to glean this information?
- Who will you ask?
- What will you do with this information when you have it? For example, you may be planning a task which requires you to script or storyboard the opening sequence of a new British crime drama. Having started with research into comparable products, you could now use a questionnaire to investigate how crime dramas target and appeal to different audiences. Which crime dramas do your respondents watch? At what time and on which channels? Is the main appeal for them the use of enigmas, the forensic or procedural detail or the relationships between the characters?

Question phrasing

Open-ended questions ask for more than a simple yes / no response and allow the respondents to compose their own answers rather than choosing between a number of given answers. For example:

1. How do you think the police are represented in crime dramas?

2. Why do you feel that crime dramas are targeting an older, educated audience?

These sorts of questions may provide more valid data, since respondents can say what they mean in their own words. However, this kind of response can also be difficult to classify and quantify, so think carefully how you will deal with a variety of different answers – and don't make the mistake of asking too many people!

With closed or fixed-choice questions, the respondent is able to choose between a number of given answers, perhaps by ticking a box or circling their answer. For example:

1. Do you think women in crime dramas are represented realistically? Yes / No.

2. How many hours a week do you watch crime programmes?

1 hour; 2–3 hours; 4 –5 hours; 6–7 hours; 8–9 hours; 10 hours+

These questions provide responses that can be easily classified and quantified.

It also requires relatively little time and effort to arrive at certain statements. However, a closed / fixed-choice question does not allow individuals to develop their own answers.

Designing a questionnaire

A well-designed questionnaire, although difficult to write initially, will help yield the information that you need. In terms of layout, you should consider the following:

- The layout should be clear and easy to read.

- Avoid jargon: you want all your respondents to feel comfortable when completing it. Remember they are giving their valuable time to you.

- Anonymity is important. Many respondents do not like putting their names on questionnaires. They do need to be made to feel that they are helping you and that no judgements will be made about them and their responses.

- Questionnaires shouldn't be too long as this may put people off completing them. Try to limit them to five or six questions and so plan them carefully.

- All spellings must be correct.

- Thank your respondents at the end of the questionnaire.

Do not be tempted to go straight to the distribution stage. It is always best to give the questionnaire a trial run. Ideally, test it on a group similar to the one that will form the main focus of your study. Ask your pilot group how long it took them to complete. Were the instructions and questions clear and unambiguous? Was the layout of the questionnaire clear? This will help you to revise the questionnaire ready for the main distribution, increasing your chances of getting useful and valid data.

Your respondents

You need to decide who you want to question and why. For example, will you only be asking boys, or certain age groups? Will you limit the survey to your college / school, your neighbourhood, your town or beyond? If you decide to limit, why are you doing this?

Finally, the results of your questionnaire should be summarised and used to inform your work.

Focus groups

Focus groups can yield very useful information, thereby making them a valid research option and, as such, focus groups can be useful both as part of your preliminary research and / or a useful forum for obtaining feedback and evaluative comments *after* you have completed your production. A focus group can be defined as a group of interacting individuals having some common interest or characteristics. The group usually contains 7–10 people.

You may decide that a focus group is a useful research method. You might therefore bring together a group of people who have stated that the horror genre is their favourite film genre. You might show the group five clips from different horror films from the 1960s to the present day looking at the representation of women in them and discussing what changes they notice in these representations. You might also want to steer the discussion with carefully scripted questions. However, you should aim to allow participants to talk to each other, ask questions and express doubts and opinions. By its nature, focus group research is open-ended and cannot be entirely pre-determined.

This style of research could provide you with invaluable data for an investigation or help you plan how you might storyboard a sequence for a new horror film.

Interviews

An interview is an interactive process involving an interviewer and a single respondent. Answers can be recorded using an MP3 player or dictaphone, or notes can be made. Using an MP3 player / dictaphone can be distracting and intimidating to respondents and you will need to ask their permission. With practice, the easiest method for respondent and interviewer is generally making informal notes.

You may decide that you wish to interview a sample of women aged between 18 and 45, to ask them questions on soaps they currently watch. Through your research you may have found that soaps are supposed to represent reality and that the audience should be able to relate to the situations and characters they view. You may wish to determine whether women can relate to the fictional female characters within soaps.

In a *schedule structured interview*, the questions and how they are worded are fixed and identical for each respondent. Therefore any differences in responses are due to the actual differences between respondents and not to the process of the interview. This reduces the chances of an interviewer influencing the responses.

A *focused* or *non-schedule structured interview* is used with respondents who have been involved in a common or particular experience. The interview poses questions referring to situations that have been analysed before the interview. The respondent is, therefore, given considerable freedom to express his or her own views. For example, you might show your respondents two film clips which might be considered violent or offensive and ask them to compare their responses to each clip. This could culminate in an investigation into different audience responses to, for example, war films.

The major advantage of conducting an interview is its adaptability. It does take some skill on the interviewer's part to know how to follow up ideas, probe questions and investigate motives and feelings, which a questionnaire can never do. The interviewer will also be looking at how the interviewee is responding to questions through, for example, their tone of voice, facial expressions, hesitation and any change of body language.

As part of these research approaches you should consider ethical issues.

The **focus group** technique was developed after the Second World War to evaluate audience responses to radio programmes. Since then, researchers have found focus groups to be useful in understanding how or why people hold certain beliefs about a topic of interest.

Ethical considerations are the same for most methods of research. For example, when you select any respondents to help you with your research, you must ensure that full information about the purpose and uses of their contributions is given. Being honest and keeping participants informed about the expectations of the group and topic and not pressurising them to speak is good practice. Another important ethical issue to consider is the handling of sensitive material and confidentiality. Participants need to be encouraged to keep confidential what they hear during the meeting and researchers have the responsibility to ensure that everyone remains anonymous. If you are recording your participants' contributions, you need to ask their permission. If you are interviewing or observing children, you *must* obtain their parents' or guardians' permission.

Once all your research has been completed and your planning activities are finished, you are ready to complete your production.

Production

A media production should reflect your very best technical ability. For print productions, generally undertaken individually, you must use your own photographic images. For audio-visual productions you must use original footage. Before you begin this work you therefore need to learn how to use the equipment available to you and then practise using it until you are confident with it!

Finally, productions don't always run smoothly and you should be prepared for yours to take time and to require revisions and modifications as you go. Read the sections below which include some practical tips for students. You can either use them or adapt them.

For print productions:

- Many student print productions are submitted with glaring typos and spelling gaffs that could have been avoided by a simple check! So always proof-read any drafts and your final production to avoid errors in spelling and expression.

- Think about your margins – students often make pages without any thought for the settings of margins. They are often too narrow so remember to set them wider in order to make the most of the space. Check what margins are commonly used in the designs of comparable products.

- Some print pages use white space as a background for their layout design. Most of the texts aimed at teenagers do not. They use blocks of colours cleverly positioned next to each other with different colour fonts over the top. Do remember to check your white space and make sure that if it is a feature of your page then it is a deliberate one.

- Make sure columns of copy are fully justified in blocks. There are a few ways of doing this, but a simple method is simply to highlight the copy and press 'control J'.

- If you decide to use coloured boxes or backgrounds, make sure your choice of font colour is sufficiently dark (or light) to be read clearly. There is no point in choosing an intense dark green background and then writing on it with blue font – it will be unreadable! Print a sample section of the page to check the font colour works with the background.

- Think carefully about the font(s) you may use. Different ones connote different messages to your audience. Try to avoid word art font styles if you can – they generally look childlike and formulaic – it is much better to use a well chosen font from the long list of *serif* and *sans serif* fonts in the word library. Make sure it is appropriate to what you are producing.

For audio-visual productions:

- Check how long your audio-visual production should be in minutes and aim to be as close to this as possible. Given your time constraints make something that is appropriate – don't try to make an epic film!

- When setting up a shot, always start recording slightly before you call 'action' and let it continue filming slightly after you call 'cut'. Think about lighting – never set up a shot with a strong light source behind your subject, it will make the shot very dark. Try to have the strongest light source behind the camera.

- Use an external microphone if you can. If you do not have one, then insist on absolute silence on set and try to avoid filming in large rooms where sound may echo. Your editing programme may also allow you to dub sections of the production after shooting. This is particularly recommended if you are making a music video.

- You may think your production makes sense in terms of its plot, but it can be difficult to make a narrative work in a very short space of time. Trial your production at an early stage with a focus group to make sure it makes sense to your intended audience!

- Use a music soundtrack with care and make sure your characters can still be heard speaking when the music begins!

Evaluating your work

All planning and production work should be evaluated – that is, critically assessed to measure its effectiveness and suitability of purpose. One useful way of doing this is to compare your final production with the comparable products you used during the planning stages. Assess the strengths and weaknesses of your finished production against the strengths (and weaknesses) of those products. You might also like to consider using questionnaires or focus groups to get audience feedback and reactions to your work. Don't be disheartened if some of the comments appear negative; assess them carefully and make suggestions as to how you could improve your own work if you were to do it again.

Evaluations vary in length and format so check with your teacher what your specification requirements are. You may be given a choice of how to present your evaluation so think carefully about which method best suits the information you want to convey. Common choices for evaluations include:

- An essay.

- An illustrated report – here you could include your initial mind map, graphs or screen grabs used in your research.

- A power point – these generally combine words, images and other types of data such as charts. They may also include customised animations, inserted images or audio-visual clips. But, a word of warning – check your required word count, as you may need to use slide notes as supplementary evidence to reach it.

- A suitably edited blog. A blog is a 'diary'-style log which could record your production 'journey' and assess its outcome. But be careful, this is still part of your assessment and it will need to be appropriate in tone and be edited to include the required material. Blogs may also contain links to other websites (hyperlinks) and original images to support the views being offered in the writing.

Use the following guide as a checklist for evaluation writing – you may not need to include all these points but they are all worth considering:

✓ Briefly explain your initial aims – what were you hoping to achieve?

✓ What comparable texts did you analyse in order to help you?

✓ Who is your target audience? What research did you undertake in order to ensure that your product was accurately targeted?

✓ What technologies did you use in the making of your product(s)? What were your strengths and weaknesses in using them?

✓ What difficulties did you have to overcome in actually producing your work?

✓ Have you tried out your production on your target audience in the form of a focus group? What was the response?

✓ Compare your own production with existing media products. Consider what you have done well and what mistakes you have made. In what ways could you have rectified these?

Finally, look carefully at your finished work. Considering (a) the planning you undertook in making it and (b) the actual production itself, what elements are you most pleased with? Take time to explain why.

End Notes

Referencing

When writing a research assignment, you will need to refer to material written or produced by others. This procedure is called citing or referencing. Consistency and accuracy are important, enabling readers to identify and locate the material to which you have referred.

It is very important that you always state where you have accessed your information. Failure to do so is an act of plagiarism, which basically means that you have stolen work from an author and have tried to pass it off as your own. Acknowledging that certain material has been borrowed, and providing your reader with the information necessary to find that source, is usually enough to prevent charges of plagiarism. All statements, opinions and conclusions taken from another writer's work must be cited, whether the work is directly quoted, paraphrased or summarised.

One referencing system you could use is the Harvard referencing system. Here, cited publications are referred to within the text by giving the author's surname and the year of publication only. The full details are then listed in a bibliography at the end of the investigation. For example:

'In a popular study, Mulvey (1975) argued that women in film are often portrayed as sexual objects for the voyeuristic pleasure of a male audience...'

This example shows how the writer has put their research into their own words but has acknowledged the source.

OR

'As Lacey (2000: 136) said, "*not all genre texts can be adequately categorised in this way*".'

In this example the student has elected to quote directly from the book.

If there are two authors the surname of both should be cited. For example:

'Branston and Stafford (1996) have proposed that...'

If there are more than two authors, the surname of the first author only should be given, followed by *et al.* (a Latin abbreviation, meaning, and others). For example:

'Audiences are said to like the concept of genre because of its reassuring and familiar promise of patterns of repetition and variation (Rayner *et al.*, 2001: 55).'

To cite from a newspaper / journal, the full date which applies must be given. For example:

'Magazine publisher IPC has launched a website for its fashion weekly *Look*, in the latest in a string of investments in digital media (*The Guardian*, 3 June 2008).'

Writing a bibliography

At the end of a piece of work, you need to list references to documents cited in the assignment. This list may be called a Bibliography or References. In the Harvard System, the references are listed in alphabetical order of authors' names. You should get into the habit of placing references in alphabetical order at the end of the assignment as you write it. For example:

- Burton, G. (2000), *Talking Television*, Arnold Publishers: London.

- Neale, Steven et al. (1998), *Hollywood Cinema*, Routledge: London.

Note the structure with the surname first, followed by a comma, then the author's first name or initials, then the year of publication, the title in italics and the publisher and place of origin.

References from the internet should give:

- The author's surname, followed by a comma and then first name or initial and year, if known.

- Title of the article.

- The web address.

- The date you first found the article on the internet.

For example:

Richards, Sarah, Why are soap operas so popular?,

http://www.aber.ac.uk/media/sections/tv09.html, (4 June 2008).

It is important when referencing from the internet that you always cite the date that you accessed the information on. The internet is forever changing and pages will disappear!

INDEX

Picture Credits

The publisher believes the following copyright information to be correct at the time of going to press, but will be delighted to correct any errors brought to our attention in future editions.

page 13 – *EastEnders* (BBC); page 16 – *Bridget Jones's Diary*, 2001 (Little Bird/Studio Canal/Working Title/Miramax/Universal) – *EastEnders* (BBC);

page 19 – *The Bill* (Thames Television/Talkback Thames/Pearson Television International) – *CSI: Crime Scene Investigation* (Jerry Bruckheimer Television/CBS Paramount);

page 21 – *Tombraider: Underworld* (Eidos Interactive/Crystal Dynamics) – *Return to Castle Wolfenstein* (Activision/Raven Software);

page 29 – *Psycho*, 1960 (Shamley Productions/Paramount) – *The Shining*, 1980 (Hawk Films/Peregrine/Producers Circle/Warner Bros.);

page 34 collage – Agyness Deyn, <shah2u.com/blog/wp-content/uploads/2008/03/marcus2.jpg>, Natasha Kaplinsky, Emily Maitlis <www.bbcchannelpartners.com> - Cristiano Ronaldo <www.cristianofans.com>,Tony Blair;

page 38 – Curdridge Primary School www.curdridge.hants.sch.uk;

page 42 – *Tombraider: Underworld* (Eidos Interactive/Crystal Dynamics);

page 46 – www.lorealparis.co.uk;

page 48 www.dolcegabbana.com;

page 49 – www.lorealparis.co.uk;

pages 50–1 – www.campaignforrealbeauty.com;

page 54 – *Closer* © 2008 Bauer London Lifestyle – *Men's Health* – National Magazine Company <www.natmags.co.uk> – *GQ Magazine* © Condé Nast Publications <www.gqmagazine.co.uk> – *Heat Magazine/Heat World* © Emap London Lifestyle <www.heatworld.com>;

page 65 – *BBC News* (BBC);

page 71 – *Skins* logos/character styles <www.e4.com/select/any.skinslogos/image/latest/watch.e4> Claire Summerlin, Alysha Davis, Chantal Oosman, Simon Helm, Steve Leek, Francesca Chen;

page 73 – *Skins* (Company Films/E4/Stormdog Films);

page 74 – *The Wire* (Blown Deadline Productions/HBO);

pages 82–3, 85 – *World of Warcraft* (Blizzard Entertainment);

page 84 – *Second Life* © Linden Research, Inc.;

page 87 – *South Park* (Comedy Central/Comedy Partners);

page 90 – GlaxoSmithKline/Eidos Interactive;

page 91 – *The Face* (Emap) <www.emap.com>;

page 93 – *Bully* (Rockstar Vancouver/Rockstar Games);

page 94 – *The O.C.* (Warner Bros./Wonderland Sound and Vision/College Hill Pictures);

pages 103 & 114 – *The Bourne Ultimatum*, 2007 (Universal Pictures/Motion Picture BETA/The Kennedy/Marshal Company/Ludlum Entertainment);

pages 105 & 114 – *Atonement*, 2007 (Working Title Films/Relativity Media/Studio Canal);

pages 108, 110 & 114 – *This is England*, 2006 (Big Arty Productions/EM Media/Film4/Optimum Releasing/Screen Yorkshire/UK Film Council/Warp Films);

page 120 – *Total Film* © Future Publishing Limited <www.totalfilm.com>;

page 122 – *Grazia* © Bauer Consumer Media <www.graziamagazine.co.uk>;

pages 124–6 – *2000AD* (IPC/Fleetway/Rebellion Developments);

page 126 – *Them!*, 1954 (Warner Bros./Warner Home Video);

page 131 – © Chanel 2004/Baz Luhrmann;

page 136 © Chanel;

page 137 – @ Beckham Fragrances/Downtown Communications <www.beckham-fragrances.com>;

page 138 – © Nike Inc.;

page 154 – © Proctor and Gamble

Notes

Notes